# THE REINTERPRETATION
# OF AMERICAN LITERATURE

# THE REINTERPRETATION
# OF AMERICAN LITERATURE

## Some contributions toward the under-
## standing of its historical development

Edited by

**NORMAN FOERSTER**
for the American Literature Group
of the Modern Language Association

Preface by

**ROBERT P. FALK**
*University of California*

*New York*
RUSSELL & RUSSELL
1959

COPYRIGHT, 1928, BY
HARCOURT, BRACE AND COMPANY, INC.
COPYRIGHT, 1955, 1959, BY
NORMAN FOERSTER

L. C. Catalog Card No.: 59-6876

PRINTED IN THE UNITED STATES OF AMERICA

# CONTENTS

# PREFACE

I<small>T</small> is not all nostalgia which draws Americans to the literary fountains of the 1920's. The originality of its writers and the fresh viewpoints of its historians and critics have marked it clearly as a decade of new beginnings in taste and opinion. The battle of the bookmen which filled the journals with opposing theories, critical attitudes, and interpretations forms an important part of the intellectual history of that time. Mencken, Van Wyck Brooks, More, Babbitt, Stuart Sherman, Randolph Bourne, and others — roving critics, literary radicals, independents, neo-humanists — all participated lustily in the general warfare of ideas. "We have never before had so many of them," wrote Norman Foerster in 1926, "or so many who were noisy, or so many shades of opinion." It was a time for revaluations, redefinitions, revolts, and reactions which we are still only beginning to sift and measure in the perspective of thirty years.

In 1928 appeared a volume of literary essays entitled *The Reinterpretation of American Literature*, edited by Foerster and written by a group of university scholars and members of the American Literature Group of the Modern Language Association. The book shared much of the critical mood of the twenties, as its title suggests, but with a certain difference. It expressed the point of view of academic critics whose special task and training is the organization and transmission of knowledge, the historical evaluation of it, and the exploration of broad areas of the past. To paraphrase the title and subtitle of the book, its purpose was to make contributions toward understanding the "historical development" of American literature. It sought to investigate the major shaping forces which had determined the character of our literature from the beginning and to accomplish for literature what historians like Turner, Osgood, Beard and others had done for social and cultural history. Likewise, the authors hoped to point out new directions or fresh perspectives which succeeding scholars might find useful in continuing research. *The Reinterpretation* was quickly recognized as "a challenge to scholarship," and during the five years of its life in print and throughout the 1930's, its influence was felt in graduate study, dissertations, textbooks, and literary histories.

The book had its origin in the work of Norman Foerster on *American Poetry and Prose* and in a paper he gave in 1925 on the major background forces of American literature. Jay B. Hubbell had written a pioneering essay on the frontier, and in discussions which followed these papers the idea developed for a collection of essays on literary history comparable to Arthur M. Schlesinger's *New Viewpoints in American History*. The authors were active in initiating the graduate study of American literature, helping to launch the new internationally-circulated periodical. *American Literature*, and encouraging historical and bibliographical research. All have since become widely known for notable works of scholarship, some of which found first expression in the chapters of *The Reinterpretation*.

The present re-issue may serve as a backward glance at travelled roads, a milestone by which we can measure the changes which have taken place in American criticism since 1928. The core of the book is its elucidation of four dominating "factors," or forces, in American thought and literary expression outlined by the editor in his opening chapter — the Puritan tradition, the frontier influence, romanticism, and realism. Other chapters were pointed towards the problem of methods, critical points of view, and the whole vexing question of the relation of literature to history and ideas. *The Reinterpretation* has now become a landmark in the changing patterns of our literary epistemology. Furthermore, it may be read today as a collection of provocative essays written in the spirit of exploration and discovery which marked the critical controversies of the mid-twenties.

Reviews of *The Reinterpretation* commented upon

x

the challenging nature of its central theme, its author-
itative tone, and its historical method of investigating
the backgrounds of American literature. Proponents
of "æsthetic" criticism hastened to state their case.
H. S. Canby acknowledged that study of the background was a necessary, though "preliminary" function of criticism, but he was concerned lest the
methods of science supersede those of intuitive and
impressionistic evaluation. "If American literature is
to be reinterpreted," he wrote, "we shall need then
more than this book provides, although we shall need
all it provides." George Whicher found the book
valuable for its "significant principles of organization" of literary materials and warned against literary
scholars taking over too readily the assumptions of
their colleagues in the social sciences. Yet Foerster had
clearly stated his awareness that the methods of historical scholarship do not always achieve their best
triumphs with superior literature, and the chapters of
*The Reinterpretation* made no pretense at performing
the function of *both* intellectual history and interpre-
tive criticism of major works.

Much research has taken place in the thirty years
since *The Reinterpretation* was first published. Time
has brought about new methods of criticism, and has
vastly enlarged the corpus of factual knowledge to be
encompassed, making the efforts to synthesize more
difficult in proportion as they become more necessary.

It is needless to say that the authors, were they to revise their essays now, would write different chapters — or, quite possibly, not write them at all — for some would have it that the "progress" of scientific knowledge has advanced beyond our ability to unify or organize it into intelligible units. But good criticism, like good literature, does not easily go out of date, and indeed, it is just as well that these essays are not revised. If we are to take a cue from its own philosophy, the values of the book can best be seen in the light of those circumstances which helped produce it.

One measure of developments from then to now may be made by comparing a recent study, *Transitions in American Literary History* (1954) with *The Reinterpretation*. This volume, like its predecessor, was a book of joint authorship published under the auspices of The Modern Language Association. In the introduction Professor H. H. Clark underlined the continued need for some broad intellectual classification and synthesis of literary knowledge and emphasized the importance of studying the "links" between the major forces which Foerster and his colleagues had first outlined. The "isms," or "norms" (as Rene Wellek has termed them), are essentially those of *The Reinterpretation* with the significant addition of "Neo-Classicism" as a descriptive term for eighteenth-century tendencies. The influence of the studies of Arthur O. Lovejoy is reflected in *Transitions* by the greater complexity of the chapters on various kinds of romanticism. Transcendentalism is treated in a separate chapter. *Transitions* brings into its pages the work of many scholars unavailable to the authors of *The Reinterpretation,* and although it gains in scope and completeness, it inevitably sacrifices something of the clear focus of the earlier volume.

The central position of literary history during the 1920's and 1930's has altered somewhat during the intervening years with the development of new critical techniques, the changing status of literature in the universities and colleges, and other factors too complex to discuss here. To mention one of the most obvious, however, the rapid growth of the great "corporations" in criticism — Melville, James, Faulkner, Eliot — has had the effect of limiting the function of full-length histories to the less critical functions of reference, definition, organization, and a large-scale mapping of national trends. The *Literary History of the United States* (1948) and *The Literature of the American People* (1951), the two most extensive collaborative histories, include many chapters on minor authors, side-currents, and social issues which one cannot find elsewhere. Generally they have abandoned or subordinated the broad intellectual patterns outlined in *The Reinterpretation* for a multiplicity of smaller chapter and division headings. These histories, and others to come, will continue to perform a highly important function, but it seems likely that as a *genre* literary history will itself become an object of analysis and will be studied and written *about* in programs devoted to critical methods.

The four major "factors" put forth with lucidity and in a spirit of inquiry by Foerster and his colleagues have provoked many a critical debate since 1928, and the energy of the controversies over such terms as "Puritanism," is testimony to the persistent need for, to quote Professor Wellek again, "tracing the sequence of periods, the rise, dominance, and disintegration of conventions and norms." The Puritan strain has been the most embattled of these "isms" perhaps because it touches so many aspects of American life outside the literary. In his lively essay in *The Reinterpretation* Kenneth B. Murdock demonstrated the affirmative elements in the Puritan tradition, and he wisely chose to emphasize its bequest to *literature* in America. He was concerned not only with the problem of definition and the work needed for clearer understanding of the historical period, but with the influence of Puritanism upon nineteenth and twentieth century writing. Penetrating studies in these directions have been written since by Perry Miller, S. E. Morison, Thomas Johnson, George Willison, William Haller, T. J. Wertenbaker, and Murdock himself. The views of such critics of Puritanism as the early Van Wyck Brooks, Mencken, and Weber have lost some of their conviction in the light of these books, and the increased literary stature of Bradford, Edwards, and Taylor and the apparent influence of Puritanism on such major writers as Hawthorne, Melville, Dickinson, Robinson, or Frost weigh strongly against the vitiating effects which it has allegedly had upon other phases of American life and letters.

Puritanism is, likewise, a part of "The European Background," a chapter in which Howard M. Jones unequivocally reminded us, at a time when criticism was still not free from provincialism (if, indeed, it is today) that our literature is a part of the western mind and should be studied not alone for its differences from, but for its homogeneity with European culture. On the other hand, nationalism and the frontier, as counterforces, are considered in Jay B. Hubbell's chapter. Hubbell, following Turner's famous thesis, summarized the nationalizing effects of the existence in America of a frontier, warning against its overemphasis for literature, "a paler, less distinct reflection of the frontier than is history." Historians have vigorously debated Turner's theory and diminished somewhat its original impact, while literary scholars have turned to such problems as Cooper, the west as myth and symbol, sources of native humor culminating in Mark Twain, western types and stereotypes. In the present struggle for world survival, cultural nationalism will necessarily play a secondary role to comparative literary study, but American literary history will continue to seek patterns in which both forces coalesce to help explain, as does the recent *Cycle of American Literature* by Robert E. Spiller, the significant achievement of our literature in the twentieth century.

Romanticism and realism (with or without capitals) belong more properly within the literary canon. They have become as essential to the scholar's vocabulary as once were "imagination" and "reason" for the Coleridgeans. In 1925, when Foerster outlined the major influences, romanticism was only beginning to be used in its intellectual sense (as in Lovejoy's article in 1924, "On the Discrimination of Romanticisms"), but only as it applied to English and European romanticism. Foerster and Paul Kaufman must be counted pioneers in a vast and complex subject for their early definitions of American romanticism. Parrington, who had published *The Romantic Revolution in America* in 1927 and was at work on *The Beginnings of Critical Realism* defined both those terms in strongly socioeconomic terms — "critical" romanticism and realism — an explanation, along with his vigorous prose style, for the great influence of those books during the 1930's. But later uses of the term "romanticism" (often reduced to its adjectival equivalent) have employed it to describe the flowering of literature in New England before the Civil War or in such variants as "American Renaissance," "Romantic Triumph," or "Romantic Rediscovery." More recently the tendency is to treat romanticism and realism in more limited relationship to the æsthetic principles of individual writers like Emerson and Melville, or Howells and James rather than in their larger intellectual sense. The general re-alignment of American literary giants which has taken place since 1920 has made these two "isms" less applicable to nineteenth-century periods and requires their redefinition in terms applicable to the twentieth-century "renaissance" as well.

A word must be said about the essays in *The Re-interpretation* which dealt more generally with the methods of literary history and criticism. These include Foerster's lucidly-written introduction with its sense of the values of literary study when carried on in a balanced proportion of synthesis and factual knowledge, the challenging "Call for a Literary Historian" of F. L. Pattee, and the stimulating approaches to critical method in the chapters by Schlesinger and Clark. The latter's essay on "Literary History and Literature" effectively countered the reservations of reviewers that the volume was not concerned with literature *per se*. Its convincing demonstration of the method by which a poem of Freneau or Melville's *Moby-Dick* could acquire larger meaning when read as if through "windows" looking back to the historical landscape marks it as an early instance of the most balanced of recent critical approaches.

The reviews in 1929 had much to say of methods and philosophies of criticism, but not enough to say of the *level* of critical intelligence and literary skill which the essays in *The Reinterpretation* uniformly demonstrated. Its republication thirty years after is some indication that a good work of criticism, regardless of its theory or philosophy or the "school" it represents, can illuminate and vitalize the literature with which it is concerned. Any one who *reads* or *re-reads* these chapters today, new critic, old critic, or middle-aged, myth-maker or symbolist, sociological or psychological scholar, will sense in them a comprehensiveness of range, a judicial tone, and a distinction of style which led a reviewer in the London *Times* to characterize the book as an illustration of the sanest and most interesting critical standards in the post-war America of the Twenties.

ROBERT FALK
Los Angeles, California
1959

# INTRODUCTION

A MONG the signs of a profounder interest in American literature is the decision of the American literature group of the Modern Language Association to publish this collaborative book, this series of articles designed to encourage and in some measure direct a fresher, more thoughtful, more purposeful approach to the understanding of our literature. What such an approach means, I wish to suggest here by reviewing and applying the opinions dominating the book, though while so doing I shall perhaps also express opinions to which some of the contributors would not lend their assent.

In the shock of the World War, thinking Americans in large measure lost the contemporaneity of mind for which they had been notorious and began to reach into the past for support and light—the past of Occidental and especially of American civilization. More recently, our increasing awareness of our world supremacy in material force has more and more evoked a sense of need of self-knowledge. In Europe, similarly, the feeling is growing that the power of America renders it perilous to remain in the dark as to what she really is.

In the universities of both America and Europe, the study of our literature as a revelation of our culture is at last being seriously undertaken. Notwithstanding a few honorable names, American scholarship and education in the field of the national letters have till recently merited shame rather than pride. In general it has been a subject attractive to facile journalists and ignorant dilettanti, and repellent to sound but timorous scholars. The time is not distant, however, when this study will be pursued in the same spirit and with the same methods employed in the study of other modern literatures.

That such a change in spirit and method will involve a reinterpretation of our literary history is, I think, demonstrated by this book. Its object is not to present striking discoveries and novel conclusions, but to suggest the spirit and manner in which a fresh interpretation should be undertaken. While a majority of the chapters are concerned, it is true, with a particular set of factors in our literary history, the contributors have dealt with this set of factors experimentally. The vagueness of our knowledge of literary history in America, the myths that remain undispelled, our feeble understanding of the lives and works of even our major authors, the large dark areas of unexplored fact that reach in many directions from the major authors, forbid an attitude of confidence in the formation of general statements. Like the contributors to the *Cambridge History of American Literature* (the first volume of which appeared in 1917, eleven years ago), our literary historians are still seriously embarrassed by the paucity of known facts in which support may be found for generalizations. Our need of facts is quite as patent as our need of penetrating generalizations. If it is obvious that facts are useless unless marshaled in generalizations, it is equally obvious that generalizations are useless unless sustained by facts.

The secular progress of knowledge in the fields of science and history, however, indicates that important acquisitions of knowledge normally *follow* the formulation of a generalization or hypothesis. A new interpretation or point of view is suddenly opened by the imagination; it appears to flood with light a host of known facts; the discoverer and his successors subject it to the test of extended exploitation, using it to direct their research. The result, at length, is the acceptance of a new conception, and, simultaneously, a large collection of significant facts previously unknown. Hence we find, in all fields of study, both workers primarily notable for insight and workers primarily notable for accurate observation, and they are not rivals but collaborators, indispensable to each other and to the task. This cooperative relation might be illustrated by the present workers in biology, physics, or any other science, or by those in history, which, as the American Historical Association has lately maintained (*The Writing of History*, 1926) partakes of the nature of art as well as of science. It could also be illustrated by the present workers in the American Literature Group of the Modern Language Association, whose interests are divergent yet inevitably harmonious. This book, therefore, concerned as it is mainly with points of view, by no means represents the total activities of the Group.

Inasmuch as scholarship and teaching are practically so closely related, something should be said here as to the academic consequences of the points of view expressed in this book, especially the consequences in the training of doctors of philosophy. At present, this training may be characterized as vague and aimless, partly because behind it lies an inadequate interpretation of American literature—if, indeed, any interpretation at all—and partly because the subject has traditionally been embraced within the department of English literature. Since every doctor in the field of American literature receives his degree through the department of English and presumably will teach in that department, it is perhaps natural that his training should be the usual one in the department—with American literature annexed either as another large field to be conquered or, more often, as a hobby that may be tolerated. In either case, his training wants the clarity and thoroughness of that in the other national literatures.

Now, while American literature cannot be termed a national literature in the usual sense, it is assuredly not a mere reflection of English literature. Since the earliest colonial days when the inhabitants of the plantations were British born and educated, American culture has become less and less "English" and more and more international, possibly also more and more native. In language alone must the cultural bond with England remain close; yet even this bond, in the opinion of some competent scholars, is weak enough already to justify the term "American language." The central fact is that American literature has had its own special conditions of development and its own special tendencies arising from these conditions. Among the literatures of the modern world, its case is unique. The culture out of which it first issued was not a native growth but a highly elaborate culture transplanted to a wilderness that receded slowly as the frontier was pushed westward. More fully than any other, American culture is derivative, and consequently the study of American literature is essentially a study of comparative literature, a study in the international history of ideas and their literary expression. It follows that the three broad problems with which

the student of American literary history is concerned
are: (1) In what sense is our literature distinctively
American? (2) In what ways does it resemble the literatures of Europe? and (3) What are the local conditions
of life and thought in America that produce these results? In the present volume, American literature is
conceived as having developed in terms of the frontier
spirit, the Puritan tradition, romanticism, and realism, a
scheme that, however far from final, suffices to indicate
the kind of background needed by the student. If his
training is to have clarity and thoroughness, it must
prepare him for a real confrontation of the nature of
American culture. He must acquire, as he does not now
acquire, a usable knowledge of the social, economic, and
political history of modern Europe, especially of England; of the history of modern philosophy and religion;
of the literature and literary history of modern Europe,
especially those of England since the Renaissance. At the
same time, and in relation to the foregoing subjects, he
must acquire a vital acquaintance with the social,
economic, and political history of America. It is possible
that in other modern literatures—in English, French,
German, etc.—background of this kind is more important than the conventional doctoral requirements would
imply; certainly, it is peculiarly important in the case of
American literature. As for the subjects in the existing

program that might most readily be sacrificed to make room for such knowledge, and as for the proper place of American literature in the departmental organization of the university—these must remain matters for future consideration.

There is current today a desire not only to reinterpret but also to revaluate American literature. We are increasingly aware of the inadequacy of some of the traditional estimates formulated in the last century, the century in which the bulk of our literature was written. Yet the new estimates tend to be capricious, indicative of a provincialism of time (the measurement of past literature by the ideas and moods of a narrow present) far more insidious than that provincialism of place from which American criticism suffered in the last century. To the problems of criticism the American scholar cannot afford to be indifferent, and for two reasons: first, because, in his capacity as teacher of college youth, he is compelled to decide what literature deserves attention on esthetic as well as historical grounds; and, secondly, because, in his capacity as literary historian, he cannot fulfill the whole of his task unless he seeks to account for the success of literary works in so far as this success is the result of their esthetic qualities. The historical scholar attains his most striking triumphs when dealing with inferior literature; this is true because his methods and instruments perhaps suffice for the explanation of such literature, while they do not suffice for the explanation of superior literature. In other words, although brief success may be accounted for by temporary and non-esthetic causes, protracted success issues from excellences that are largely timeless and esthetic, and permanent success from excellences that are wholly so. In proportion to the excellence of the literature, therefore, is the historian's need of the capacity to explain its origin, public reception, and literary influence by means of the instruments of criticism. A thoroughgoing historian must also be a critic. Hence, as we deplore criticism unconcerned with knowledge, so must we deplore knowledge unconcerned with criticism. In practice, indeed, it would be difficult to name any works of distinction in biographical or more general literary history that do not obviously employ critical standards—derivative or novel, central or eccentric, firmly or flaccidly conceived, they are inevitably present. Too seldom, however, is the scholar really aware of the standards he employs, and of the sources whence he derived them; too seldom does he devote to them the earnestness which he is wont to devote to concrete items of knowledge; too seldom is he aware that critical standards are not more liable to repeated and unending revision than interpretative generalizations and concrete facts; too seldom, in a word, is he aware of the incompleteness of his vision of history.

That the field of literary history has steadily widened, that the nineteenth-century conceptions of its scope have proved inadequate, should hereafter be made amply manifest in our guidance of graduate students. Especially should it be made clear to them that whatever potentialities of esthetic insight and of criticism they may possess are not irrelevant but indispensable to their highest achievement. They should no longer go forth from the universities, as they now too frequently do, in the belief that their task is no more than the determination and collection of facts, and that facts of whatever sort are worthy of blind pursuit. This is not to say that we are to encourage vagueness and dilettantism, or to train all our students to excel in literary criticism. It means simply that we should demonstrate to them that literary scholarship is a whole of which all the parts are related and indispensable, and that if they can eventually pass beyond the preliminary labors—the mastery of texts, the understanding of background, the description of phenomena in the growth of literature—to the delicate processes of interpretation and of criticism, they will realize at last that the life of scholarship is not a mechanism to be manipulated but indeed a life to be lived.

N. F.

# THE REINTERPRETATION
# OF AMERICAN LITERATURE

# I. A CALL FOR A LITERARY HISTORIAN [1]

## FRED LEWIS PATTEE

I HAVE nearly a hundred histories of American literature on my shelves, and I am still adding more—a
hundred volumes to tell the story of our literary century, and all of them alike, all built upon the same
model! I think I could dictate one to a stenographer in
three days, with no reference to authorities save for
dates: Colonial Period, Revolutionary Period, Knickerbocker Period, New England Period, and so on. Always
there is the same list of authors, beginning with Captain
John Smith, Anne Bradstreet, and Cotton Mather. A
few are treated in chapters by themselves: Franklin,
Irving, Bryant, Cooper, Emerson, Hawthorne, Whittier,
Longfellow, Holmes, Poe, Lowell, and, of late, Whitman
and Mark Twain. The rest are assorted into groups
according to chronology, geography, or literary forms.

But the really stereotyped thing about these histories
is their critical method: always the same list of biographical facts with emphasis upon the picturesque, always
the repetition of a standard series of well-worn myths.

[1] Reprinted from *The American Mercury*, June, 1924, with the permission of the editors.

Irving is always genial and sunny, always loyal to his lost boyhood sweetheart, Matilda Hoffman—so loyal, indeed, that he mourns her in bachelorhood to the day of his death—inexpressibly touching! Poe is always first of all the drunkard; a gruesome genius, author of "The Raven" and "The Bells," a critic lashing his enemies and praising his worthless friends; finally, the maker of the most horrible tales in the whole range of American literature. Tenderly the myths settle over Longfellow and Whittier; not so tenderly over Cooper and Whitman.

Almost all of these histories are textbooks. With the exception of John Nichol's now antiquated volume, which was written primarily for the *Encyclopædia Britannica,* and *The Cambridge History of American Literature,* which is not a history at all but a series of essays and bibliographies by a varied assortment of writers, and D. H. Lawrence's startling *Studies in Classic American Literature,* all of them have been written with classroom intent. Even Tyler's volumes on the Colonial and Revolutionary periods were first put on paper as lectures to college students. Special purpose and provincial prejudice wave over every one of them like red flags. One may arrange their authors in groups. There is, first, the New England group, headed by the Victorian Charles Francis Richardson, and later by Barrett Wendell, whose bulky *Literary History of America* should have been entitled *A Literary History of Harvard University, with Incidental Glimpses of the Minor Writers of America.* In every volume produced by this group the Transcendental Movement requires a full chapter, looming almost as large as the Reformation in European history. Often there is an additional chapter on "The New England Renaissance." Next comes a group of Southern histories, some of them frankly bearing the title, *Literature of the South.* This region has always been peculiarly sensitive, peculiarly eager to make the most of its scanty literary annals. In all its books Simms, Cooke, Timrod, Hayne, Lanier, and the after-the-war school of novelists (with scant mention of Cable), are made of major importance. Between the two extremes lies a belt stretching from Philadelphia and New York westward across the continent. Its textbooks all present close-up treatments of local celebrities, and the space required for them is taken from the New England section. A history that does not devote adequate attention to Lew Wallace and Riley and Tarkington is berated by Indiana, one that neglects Eugene Field, William Vaughn Moody and the new Illinois school of poets is scorned by Chicago, and to refuse major honors to Mark Twain, Bret Harte, Ambrose Bierce, and O. Henry is to be unwelcome in California and the Southwest.

It is high time, I believe, for a history of *American* literature to be written, and I venture herewith to suggest the fundamental ten commandments for the making of it.

First, it must be written primarily as a history, with no thought of class-room use. If professors *can* use it as a textbook let them, but it must be as detached from class-room thinking as is D. H. Lawrence's amazing volume. It must not be academic and timid, and bound fast to old critical conceptions, but on the other hand it must not be primarily iconoclastic and revolutionary, with a devastating thesis to be defended, as is the case with Van Wyck Brooks's *The Ordeal of Mark Twain*.

Second, it must be impartial and unprovincial. The writer must be completely free from sectional bias: he must be American rather than Eastern or Southern or Western. A foreigner might have the requisite detachment for the job, but he would hardly have enough understanding of the American soul, or sufficient knowledge of the whole mass of American writings. The Scotch John Nichol's *American Literature*, the most detached history thus far published, falls fatally short at more than one vital point. The work that is wanted cannot be done by a New Englander unless he has been long resident in other sections of the United

States, and it cannot be done by a Westerner or a Southerner who has not lived for some years in the New England environment. The writer will fail completely unless he is able to see his subject in the light of *all* America, from the beginning of the Colonial era.

Third, the new historian must adapt himself to the new perspective, and readjust the focus of all his optical apparatus, especially that part furnished by his academic training. We are still near the nineteenth century, in which lies the major part of our literary product, and by the old university standards nothing in that century is ready for final appraisal or even preliminary survey; nevertheless, a viewpoint gained by standing one quarter up the ladder of the new century certainly should furnish a perspective that will allow us to revise greatly the old charts. Large areas of our literary domain have not been changed as to boundary since the making of the first surveys, but we can see now over the underbrush, and the elevations are beginning to show their true heights. Is Bryant still, as of old, worth a whole chapter, or is he to be merely a part of the chapter treating Halleck and Dana and Drake? Are Cooper and Poe and Whitman isolated and towering peaks or mere bluffs? Are the New England poets a mountain range or a group of foothills? We have seen of late a sudden change in the estimate of Melville: which valuation is right, the old or the new? Are there other variables in the American firmament? Has the time come to make a new chart?

Fourth, the myths must be stripped from our major writers and they must be made to stand in the light of truth. Our critics and historians have been handicapped heretofore by want of materials, and quite naturally. It takes years for all the data about an author to be gathered and examined. We are not yet sure that we have found out, even now, all that is worth knowing about Shakespeare. He who is very near his subject is liable to be very far indeed from the ultimate truth. We still know only too little about our nineteenth century writers. The families and friends of these men, in many cases, have felt that letters, journals and the like were peculiarly precious, and have thus guarded them with vigilance. A literary executor has been appointed in each case, or an official biographer, and he commonly deems it incumbent upon him to create a myth, to surround his subject with a favoring atmosphere by making judicious selections from the mass before him, passing rapidly over lean areas, lingering long over rich areas, and arranging the whole so that a well-rounded unity appears—a mythical figure that dominates all succeeding biographies. The life of Longfellow by his brother is three pots of honey, and Higginson's is a fourth. No adequate biography of the poet has yet appeared. To one who has read them all, he is a kind of hero of the romantic order seen dimly through an atmosphere uniformly mellow and vague, like a day of Indian Summer—all harshness, all unpoetic reality lost in the dreamy haze. The papers and literary remains of Irving, Hawthorne, Emerson, Holmes, Whittier, Lowell, to name only major figures, all passed into the guardianship of their families or their friends, and no one has had access to them without strict supervision. The only life that has been at all adequately studied is Poe's, and this study has been rendered possible by the fact that Poe had no family and no friends, and that his papers, with the curious exception of the guarded letters in the "Poe Shrine," have been from the first "in the public domain."

The case of Washington Irving may be taken as typical. Of late most of his papers and journals have been surrendered by his heirs to the auction rooms, and at least three volumes of them have been published for the first time. As a result a new Irving is beginning to appear, an Irving seen without the aid of his nephew Pierre, and at times the figure is startlingly unfamiliar. It leads us to wonder what the story of American literature will look like when all the documents are fully in. The Irving papers, in Pierre's biography, were not only carefully chosen; they were actually tampered with. In his minutely-kept Dresden journal Irving records minutely day by day his growing infatuation for Emily Foster. But his proposals of marriage—evidently there were two—are forbidden us, though they were recorded by Irving, for some hand, doubtless Pierre's, has gone through the diary and carefully erased the record of them—not enough, however, to conceal the fact that Emily rejected him at least twice. The pathetic story of the heart-broken bachelor disappears. Sentimental America, of course, should never know this, for it would shatter one of its cherished myths! Again, when recently the papers of John Howard Payne were found in Tunis they revealed one of the most remarkable love-stories in the history of our literature. The widow of Percy Bysshe Shelley, Mary Godwin, became enamored of Irving and wished with her whole intense soul to marry him. She used Payne as a go-between and for a long time fully expected to be successful. Irving's side of the romance we do not know, for his letters we do not have, but certainly no woman expects daily that a man is about to propose to her without having, in some degree at least, been given cause. These instances I cite simply to show how little we really know about the actual life of some of our principal American writers.

But fresh material is appearing rapidly now. Emerson's and Thoreau's complete journals have been published; the Cooper family have disregarded ancestral wishes and published all the remaining papers of the novelist; practically all of Walt Whitman is now in sight; and there are promised new and revealing letters from others of the major group. The time seems propitious for the new historian.

His fifth commandment is that his survey must be written against the background of American history. Every author is a product of his times, and is molded by his times. Longfellow is Longfellow because, in the words of Howells, "he accepted the sole conditions on which poetry at the time could embody itself." He but voiced "the contemporary mood."

Our literature between 1800 and 1870 had three distinct centers. First was Philadelphia, aristocratic, Anglocentric, utterly intolerant of the mob, holding with its *Port Folio,* for the first quarter of the century at least, the literary leadership of America. To Dennie, its first dominating literary voice, American democracy was a thing utterly of the devil: "So far from courting the mob, our editors should treat the herd of swine and their feeders with the most ineffable contempt, and be satisfied with the general applause of scholars and gentlemen, men of honor and cavaliers." This was the voice of Philadelphia. To the north was Boston, the Edinburgh of literary America, righteous overmuch, intolerant, insulated, self-sufficient, contemptuous of all light literature, even to the ejecting of the frivolous N. P. Willis, who had dared to publish within the sacred bounds a journal wholly of this world—Boston with its ponderous *North American Review*. Never has New England produced any novels of note save Hawthorne's and Mrs. Stowe's. Even *Uncle Tom's Cabin* could not have been written without the author's saving seventeen years in Ohio. *The Scarlet Letter* stole into New England furtively, from around the pulpit. Was it not in reality a moral tract? Always the novel has had to penetrate New England in disguise. Holmes's thin fiction sneaked in through his doctor's office; Ware's through his minister's study; Longfellow's from behind his professor's chair. Midway between Boston and Philadelphia was New York—cosmopolitan, tolerant, worldly. Light literature flourished from the first in its unpuritanical atmosphere. Boston would have smothered at birth both Irving and Cooper. Willis found a congenial atmosphere in Manhattan instantly, and so did Bryant and Halleck. There followed Stedman and Stoddard and the other exiles for whom the New England atmosphere was too thin and ozoneless. The new historian must treat these three diverse areas, not separately, as if he were dealing with three independent nations, but as parts that blend into a unity—early nineteenth century America.

But he must go further. "Europe," declared Emerson in the mid-century, "extends to the Alleghanies." Cis-Alleghany America was, in those early days, a moon lighted by Europe. The Atlantic seaboard from the first had been in constant contact with the old world. Those who read anything read English books and magazines and even newspapers. The ruling class was severely aristocratic. Of the first forty years of the Republic, thirty-two saw Virginia patricians ruling and eight the Adams family of Boston. Of the first six presidents all but Washington had served at European courts. Before 1829 the East was democratic only in name. But trans-Alleghany America knew nothing of Europe, nor cared. The men of that vast empire were of the second wave of the American settlement; they had cut all eastern ties when they crossed the mountains. The Atlantic could be crossed without great difficulty, but not so the land ocean that separated the East from the West. It was a barrier like a Chinese wall, and behind it grew up a wild new race of men to whom freedom was a religion and self-dependence an axiom. They evolved a new outlook upon life, a new humor, a new conception of literature untouched by Europe. The East ignored them. Once during the Revolution the Atlantic cities became aware of them, when they burst over the mountains and fought the battle of King's Mountain, and again during the War of 1812, when they made themselves felt at New Orleans. But it was not until 1829 that the East was really awakened by their war whoop. Then it was that Jackson defeated the crown prince of the Adams family, the professor of rhetoric at Harvard College, and a new era began. No historian of American literature can blink the tremendous fact that the New England school of writers gathered and did its earliest work amid the shouting and the vulgarity of the reign of Andrew Jackson.

Unluckily, the formative thirties and forties have never been adequately studied. It was the age of the annuals, of *Godey's Lady's Book,* of *Peterson's* and *Graham's.* It was, to quote Hawthorne, the age of "a damned mob of scribbling women" that nearly drove all masculine men out of the literary field. One cannot understand Poe until one projects him against his background of sensibility and lurid adjectives. All of his earlier tales were blasts of satire—it is foolishness to weigh them in any other scales. His earlier criticism was vitriolic in its condemnation of the effeminate stuff of his day. His review of Fay's syrupy novel *Norman Leslie* is one of the most annihilating in our literature; it should be set up as a model in schools. He lashed

Longfellow, the literary idol of the forties—the Longfellow who was writing, in 1840, "I have a great notion
of working upon the *people's* feelings." He lashed him
for writing poetry with books open about him rather
than life. Poe has been fully justified in his criticism,
though the voicing of it cost him the friendship of New
England and made him an outcast.

The new historian will find the Civil War another
vital fact in our literary history. Its greatest figure was
another Western democrat risen from the mob. It destroyed New England as completely as it did the South.
Two aristocracies simultaneously fell into ruins. Following it there flooded into the East a second wave of
Western vulgarity, a new humor, a new literary form—
the native type of short story—a new realism that
scorned Europe and the East, a new poetry, the Pike
county ballad, a blow in the face of the older makers of
poetry. Then followed a debauch of dialect, local color,
Rileyism, and literary lawlessness that shocked the old
school into silence. The era of Mark Twain had dawned.
Literature began to spring from life, from the people,
from the spirit of the epoch. To separate it from its era
and to neglect its background is completely to misun-
derstand it.

Sixth, the new historian must struggle with the un-
settled question as to whether or not literature is really

possible in a democracy. The older historians, such as Richardson, defined it so as to exclude all save *belles-lettres*, the aristocratic area of the art. Others, like Wendell, have viewed the field through the atmosphere of the college lecture-room. Higginson, writing on the rise of American literature, began his study with the founding of the *Atlantic Monthly!* The title of the new history should be *A Literary History of the American People*. Such a history has never been written.

The literature of a nation flows always in at least two currents, the upper and the lower, the literary and the subliterary. In America there have really been three— the aristocratic with Richardson and Wendell as its recorders; the popular, touched very briefly by a few historians; and the submerged, totally unrecorded. At times the second current has been more evident than the clearer stream that should have been the dominating tide. It burst out with violence in the mid-century with its *Uncle Tom's Cabin*, its Fanny Fern books, its *Wide, Wide World* and *Lamplighter*, and Bonner's *Ledger*. In the seventies it reappeared in J. G. Holland, E. P. Roe and Eggleston. Today we have as typical figures Harold Bell Wright and Zane Grey, subliterary but read by astonishing numbers. The third tide, that of the dime novels and the Bertha M. Clay sentimentality, the new historian cannot neglect. It has reëmerged of late in the moving picture and in the colored Sunday magazine of the daily papers. To dismiss this current as unimportant is to refuse to write the literary history of the American people. To study only the literature of aristocracy is to be ignorant of America, for America, taking all its elements together, is synonymous with vulgarity. Cooper, in 1838, wrote:

The tendency of democracies is, in all things, to mediocrity, since the tastes, knowledge and principles of the majority form the tribunal of appeal. This circumstance, while it certainly serves to elevate the average qualities of a nation, renders the introduction of a high standard difficult. Thus do we find in literature, the arts, architecture and in all acquired knowledge, a tendency in America to gravitate toward a common centre in this as in other things; lending a value and estimation to mediocrity that are not elsewhere given.

Cooper was an aristocrat, and he went down at last after a running fight with the vulgarity of democracy. What has been the effect of attempting to educate the *whole* American mass, to make the reading of books a universal accomplishment? It has raised to a certain degree the general level of the mass, but has it not done so by lowering all the upper levels? Our literature has gone *down* to the mass.

Seventh, the new historian must throw away all the

older histories, with their Knickerbocker and New England periods, and find truer lines of cleavage. The Colonial period might be dismissed entirely, so far as its actual literary product is concerned, but it must be studied nevertheless with minuteness since it was the crucible in which was evolved the America we know. Even more so was the epic period of the Revolution. Here for the first time we find really American writing, the beginnings of our original literature, scanty perhaps—too scanty, indeed, to justify Tyler's bulky volume—yet nevertheless significant. And then came the first generation of the republic, 1790-1830, enormously important. It was the period of beginnings: of the earliest fiction—curiously enough, produced in Boston, and fiercely suppressed—of the feeble beginnings of criticism, never yet adequately studied; of national songs, volumes of them, culminating at last in the "The Star-Spangled Banner"; of ebullient democracy held firmly in check by aristocracy; of fervid Fourth of July orations, hundreds of them cast into print; of American epics made to match Niagara and the Rocky Mountains and the Great Plains; of the amazing sensations of *The Sketch Book* and Cooper's *Spy;* of dreams of an independent American literature set forth in dozens of articles and Phi Beta Kappa orations. It was the seed time; not the harvest.

Then followed the second generation of the republic —the period of tumultuous democracy—the era of Andrew Jackson, followed by the wild Tippecanoe, log cabin and hard cider era. The mob was in the saddle, and unbridled individualism was king. In literature the period was opened by Knapp's *Lectures on American Literature*, 1829, the first attempt at a history of our letters, and by *Godey's Lady's Book*, 1830. It was the era of the annuals, over a thousand different titles; the era of embellishments sentimental beyond belief, of steel engravings, and the Tom Moore-General Morris variety of gushing songs; the era of New England, transcendentalized, snobbish, absorbed in itself or looking eastward to Europe, journeying West only to deliver lyceum lectures for the culture of the barbarians, expending itself in abolitionism and fantastic reform— Alcott, Sumner, Emerson, Whittier; it was the period of spread-eagle oratory and Websterian eloquence; of the Missouri Compromise, the Kansas and Nebraska bill, and the Dred Scott decision; the age of John Brown, and of the inevitable conflict. Out of this maelstrom of vulgarity and passion and yearning came Poe and Whitman, Hawthorne and Holmes. Then with the sixties crashed the Civil War and out of it issued a new America, as hot metal from the furnace ore.

Eighth, the new historian must be a literary critic of

poise and acuteness, for if American literature has suffered from any single inadequateness that inadequateness has been in its criticism. Until recently, we have
had so few real authors that they have had praise out
of all proportion to their worth. Poe was the only real
critic during the mid-century; he stood alone. Longfellow and the New Englanders took his criticisms as
brutal abuse and after a gentle protest ignored him as
one ignores a pole-cat. Today we realize that Poe was
right. Applying modern measurements, we find the
Harvard bard vastly shrunken where his own generation found him great. The new historian will strip
away all his voluminous translations, and all his elaborate dramas; he will throw into the discard most of
the ballads of the "Tales of a Wayside Inn" variety,
and leave him at last, possibly with "Evangeline," surely
with "Hiawatha" and a few of the early ballads and
lyrics, and unquestionably with the sonnets, which are
one of the glories of American literature. Lowell, too,
may fare hard at the hands of the new critic. His criticism, once ranked as America's best, is now seen to be
intolerably smart and high-flown and over-ornate; his
odes, with the exception of a few passages, no longer
have any power; his once vaunted "Biglow Papers"
must be turned into the department of history as "original sources," not poetry: and his list of lyrics grows

shorter with every decade. A few of his essays may endure, perhaps, "Democracy" and "A Certain Condescension" and "Old Cambridge," but no more. Lowell's influence was greater than his writings. He was a Janus figure caught midway between two generations and standing comfortably with neither.

The new literary historian must be fearless, undeterred by mere reverence and influenced by no prejudice. Time has smoothed the way for him. Much that was proudly hailed by its first readers as pure gold already has gone the rubbish way to oblivion. Many historians still hold to that dead stuff, but the time has come when it must be cut away without reservation. Other critical problems remain. The mighty influence of Scott down to 1830 must be weighed, and then that of Dickens; the place occupied by the drama must be ascertained, a subject thus far almost entirely ignored by literary historians; the curious use of the Indian in American poetry and romance must be studied (at one time he was believed to be America's literary salvation!); and an inquiry must be made into the effect during most of the century of the lack of international copyright.

Ninth, the new history must show clearly the evolution and the spread of the American magazine, an institution peculiarly American and peculiarly influential in the development of our literature. Poe made it a central fact in his criticism, at least in his criticism of our prose. From the magazine emerged the American short story, the essay in many of its varieties, and to a certain extent that unique entity called American humor. Historians almost all have neglected this vital force.

Tenth and last, the new historian must be himself a writer of force and beauty, with a style simple and clear, able to master his multitudinous findings and bring them into appropriate compass, not in the dry-as-dust lecture form, but in chapters thoroughly readable. The task before him, obviously, is no easy one. Our literary growth has not been at all like that of most other nations: it has not been a steady growth from within outward; it has been rather the reverse. Our literature is a thing of shreds and patches. There was Longfellow in the thirties deliberately grafting us upon the decaying stub of the German *Sturm und Drang*, there was Irving who, instead of depicting our own *Sturm und Drang*, deliberately turned us to eighteenth century English classicism and arabesque romance; there were Willis and all the other travelers turning our eyes constantly to picturesque Europe; and later there was Harte interpreting the California gold mines in terms of Charles Dickens. The result of it all has been that our American literature is something different from anything else in the world.

## II. FACTORS IN AMERICAN LITERARY HISTORY [1]

### NORMAN FOERSTER

THE conventional mold in which our books and our college courses on American literature are cast indicates that we are not using intelligently the accelerated interest in our literature. We are still thinking in terms of a conception attained about a quarter of a century ago, despite the fact that it was superficial and premature. It is time for us to abandon the paradox involved in our theory that American literature is only a branch of English literature while in practice we treat it as a thing apart. It is time for us to abandon the political and geographic terminology in which we have enshrouded our confusion. The Colonial Period, The Revolutionary Period, The Early National and Later National Periods (or First National, Second National, etc., as if our subject were banks), The East, The West,

[1] Read before the American Literature Group of the Modern Language Association in Chicago, December 27, 1925; published, with the title "American Literature," in *The Saturday Review of Literature*, April 3, 1926; reprinted as a brochure, with the title *New Viewpoints in American Literature*, by Houghton Mifflin Company in 1926. Here reprinted with the permission of the editor of *The Saturday Review of Literature*.

The South, The New England Group, Knickerbocker
Group, Later New York Group, etc., etc.—these facile
terms totally fail to make plain the organic relation of
American and European literature, or even that the subject we are dealing with *is* literature. In a few quarters
there has been, since the war, an enthusiastic waving of
the flag "Americanism"; but obviously those who rally
round this stirring symbol have commonly but the
faintest idea of what it symbolizes. It is time for us to
seek, in all simplicity and honesty, a more nearly adequate conception of American literature than has yet
existed. Throwing our nineteenth century into clearer
perspective, the Great War removed from large numbers of Americans the sectional spectacles that had distorted their vision. We are now ready for free and fresh
thought, for scientific thought, for the undisturbed use
of observation, reason, and imagination.

We have a very special opportunity, moreover, owing
to the work of recent American historians. Although
literary history is of course only a department of general history, we have egregiously failed to keep pace
with the historians. Their modification or rejection of
old points of view and introduction of new ones started
more than thirty years ago, synchronously with the
revolt in life and literature that began in the 1890's and
is still in full career. Men like Turner, Andrews,

Osgood, Adams, and Beard have given us a new vision of the forces dominant in our past. By 1922 it was possible for Professor Schlesinger to publish a book entitled *New Viewpoints in American History*, bringing together some of the results of this re-interpretation. It is time for our literary historians at least to look forward to a book of *New Viewpoints in American Literary History*.

We should also derive stimulation—perhaps some light—from the critics of American culture, or rather the critics who have been deploring the absence of "Civilization in the United States." Although we have long had such critics (including Emerson, Whitman, and other 100 per cent Americans), we have never before, I imagine, had so many of them, or so many who were noisy, or so many shades of opinion, or so many readers who applauded or reviled. While our creative energy has expressed itself in Spoon Rivers and Main Streets, our critical energy has naturally expressed itself in Prejudices, Definitions, Americans, Roving Critics, Letters and Leadership, Histories of Literary Radicals. Divine or not, ours is a discontent more insistent and comprehensive than any we have hitherto experienced in this country. The open or experimental mind—even perhaps the empty mind—has never been so widely popular "in the best circles." We are questioning everything, including things that are unquestionable. It is time for us to question our inherited conception of American literature, which is certainly not unquestionable.

I have indicated what seems to me the cardinal symptom of our disordered interpretation of American literature, namely, our tendency to think in terms of political and geographic divisions.[2] I purpose to offer a different conception, not with a view to settling offhand so large a problem, but merely to render the problem itself clearer and to suggest the spirit in which it should be approached.

*All* the factors may be comprised under two heads: European culture and the American environment. American history, including literary history, is to be viewed as the interplay of these two tremendous factors, neither of which has been studied profoundly by our literary scholars. Because they are tremendous, however, they must be divided into a serviceable number of lesser factors, and from such a list (which I must leave hypothetical) I will select the four that seem to me most important. They are (1) the Puritan tradition, (2) the

---

[2] It is obvious, however, that they are not to be wholly disregarded. The ablest statement of their significance that I have seen is an article, not by a literary historian but by F. J. Turner, "Geographic Sectionalism in American History," in *Annals of the Association of American Geographers*, June, 1926.

frontier spirit, (3) romanticism, and (4) realism. I can merely sketch their significance.

First, *the Puritan tradition*. This is, of course, only part of a larger factor, viz., the European tradition as it appeared before our Revolution. For we must reckon not only with the Puritan but also with the so-called "Cavalier" tradition, indeed the whole Anglo-Saxon tradition—its habit of mind in matters social, legal, political, economic, esthetic, religious. We must reckon with the rationalism and sentimentalism of the eighteenth century. I have selected the Puritan tradition as probably the outstanding factor in the first century and as a shaping force in the entire development of American civilization down to the present day. No doubt the Quakers, as Dr. Canby has recently asserted (*Saturday Review*, January 2, 1926), "have been neglected as a shaping force"; yet I think we are essentially right in our belief that the Protestant stamp on American life was primarily Puritan. The great problem is, rather, in just what ways Puritanism affected American life, and for the solution we must look mainly to the historians, who have not yet dealt adequately with our religious history.

Secondly, *the frontier spirit*, or (to name this factor in its broadest significance) nature, physical America. While the influence of Puritanism has been amply conceded (though never really demonstrated) by our students of literature, the influence of the frontier has been strangely neglected.[3] Professor Turner's paper on "The Significance of the Frontier in American History" presented in 1893, as Jay B. Hubbell has observed, "has wellnigh revolutionized the study of American history. . . . Yet the literary history of the frontier is still to be written." Whoever writes it will have occasion to follow the steps of Buckle, Shaler, Turner, and Paxson. Since Turner it has been clear that "the most American thing in all America" is the frontier. From Europe we derived Puritanism and, later, romanticism and realism; but the frontier is American—is the key to the definition of "Americanism." In race and tradition we are fundamentally European; but our geography is our own, and the consequences of our geography can scarcely be exaggerated. More truly than Shakespeare's England did America find herself set apart:

> This other Eden, demi-paradise,
> This fortress built by Nature for herself
> Against infection and the hand of war,
> This happy breed of men . . .

The first momentous result of this splendid isolation was political independence, which provided us henceforth

---

[3] It would now (1928) be truer to say that the influence of the frontier has been strangely exaggerated.

with an ever-stimulating sense of an heroic past and a large if not wholly manifest destiny. Isolation led to the Monroe Doctrine, which extended the boundaries of the Garden of Eden to Patagonia. As generation followed generation, the frontier in North America shifted westward, ever renewing itself and ever sending back to the East currents of thought and feeling and power that in large measure determined the development of American democracy. It transformed the European type into such men as Jefferson, Jackson, Lincoln, Roosevelt, or, among the writers, Emerson, Whitman, Mark Twain. It was Emerson who said that "Europe stretches to the Alleghanies; America lies beyond," and it was he who spoke for the frontier, as well as for romanticism, in his address on the American Scholar and his essay on Self-Reliance. The pioneer spirit is as vital in him as are his Puritan background and his kinship with Wordsworth, Coleridge, and Carlyle. In Whitman, the frontier background of Emerson's idealism becomes foreground. "Here is action untied from strings, magnificently moving in masses": and he sought to create an equivalent poetry. Nothing of Europe here—effete feudal Europe—but instead the primal virtue of the unexhausted West. The imagination of Whitman dwelt with rapture on this other Eden, this truly New World in which a happy breed of men might make a new start:

Have the elder races halted?
Do they droop and end their lesson, wearied over there beyond
    the seas?
We take up the task eternal, and the burden and the lesson,
                Pioneers!   O pioneers!

Whitman's years, 1819-92, cover the flowering and
fading of the pioneer spirit; the year of his death co-
incides almost exactly with the passing of the physical
frontier. Both Emerson and Whitman had witnessed,
with mingled feelings, the materialistic splendor that
followed the frontier. America, as Emerson viewed it,
was another name for Opportunity, and opportunity,
to most Americans from the Puritan days onward, had
meant above all economic opportunity. The conquest of
nature by man was succeeded by the conquest of man
by nature. More and more, Things were in the saddle,
as Emerson saw. "The largeness of the nation," said
Whitman even before the great era of industrial expansion, "were monstrous without a corresponding
largeness and generosity of the spirit of the citizen."
But instead of seeking such a growth of the spirit (for
which both Emerson and Whitman steadfastly offered
light and leading), America gave herself up, with slight
compunction, to materialism—a materialism colored
with a conventional religiosity, which effected the
ascendency of middle-class philistinism. The chosen race

became the children of darkness. The currents of thought and feeling and power that the frontier minority had sent back to the East steadily dwindled, and instead of working out a new national culture under the inspiration of the pioneer spirit, all America lapsed into the comfortable prosperity and philistine tyranny of Main Street.

From the early days, the absence of a national culture had been a problem and a challenge. Political and economic independence could not wholly stifle higher cravings. Necessarily, a frontier people found themselves provincial, and their provincialism took two opposite forms. On the one hand was provincial dependence, a reliance upon the cultural mother across the seas; on the other, provincial self-assertion, a narrow Americanism that extolled itself and depreciated the foreign. And the two forms could coexist in the same person. It would be interesting to discuss the diverse ways in which this problem has been envisaged by recent critics like Van Wyck Brooks, Randolph Bourne, H. L. Mencken, Stuart Sherman, and Henry Canby. I can only remark here, however, that these critics are dealing with a problem that had its origin on the frontier, that they belong in a long succession of critics and creative writers who have been concerned with it, and that they must pass on to future generations of critics and creative writers a problem that, among all the great nations, confronts America alone, because America alone is a frontier nation.

I come now to the third factor, European *romanticism*, which, like the frontier, has been strangely neglected. Despite casual glances at English romanticists, our literary historians have obscured the fact that the literature of the United States from the birth of the nation to the twentieth century is part of the Romantic Movement. We too had our precursors in the eighteenth century, of whom Freneau is the most distinguished; we had our sentimental preparation, our Werther fever, our Gothic enthusiasms, our fresh interest in nature, and we had a democratic Revolution before the French. We had our first generation of moderate romantics, writers like Bryant, Irving, and Cooper. At the height of our romantic movement, say between 1830 and the Civil War, we had the group of writers—Emerson, Hawthorne, Thoreau, Longfellow, Lowell, Whittier, Poe, Whitman, etc.—who virtually created American literature. We had in the *Blütezeit* of New England a larger and more compact "school" than the Lakists or Cockneys in England, comparable, rather with the *romantische Schule* in Germany. For inspiration we looked to England and the Continent, as England had looked to Germany, and Germany to France (or Rousseau). We had our lovers of beauty; we were fascinated by the Middle Ages; we wrote ballads; we had disciples of nature; we turned to the national past, to the Indians, the Puritans, and the Revolution; we cultivated the sense of wonder, the supernatural, the grotesque, the ego, the genius; we were ardent in social reform, and carried out pantisocratic notions at Brook Farm and Fruitlands; we worked out new theories of poetry and art in revolt against pseudo-classicism; we were reverently appreciative of Shakespeare, traveled much in the realms of Elizabethan gold, discovered or rediscovered Homer, Plato, Dante, Calderon, Rousseau, Goethe, Kant, and the Germans generally. And at length we had our decadence in Bayard Taylor, Stoddard, Stedman, Aldrich, Lanier, etc.

As in every country that experienced the romantic impulse, the movement was modified by national conditions. When Cabot said that Transcendentalism was "romanticism on Puritan soil," he might have extended his definition by saying that American literature in the nineteenth century was romanticism "on Puritan and pioneer soil." For temporal background, our romanticism has not only the Revolutionary idealism but also the Puritan idealism, an indefeasible possession: for spatial background, our romanticism looks beyond the Alleghanies to the free West. Furthermore, national conditions of more than one kind caused the romantic wave to attain its height nearly a half century later than in England and Germany. When Wordsworth, after living on into an alien age, died in 1850, our Cooper still had one year to live, Irving nine years, and Bryant twenty-eight; and these are our earliest important writers. Again, within the years 1803-19, the English writers who were born include such names as Tennyson, Browning, Thackeray, Dickens, and George Eliot, whom we are accustomed to term Victorians; but the American writers born within the same years are Emerson, Hawthorne, Longfellow, Whittier, Poe, Thoreau, Lowell, and Whitman, our outstanding romantics. And again, the Victorians died, on the average, before the American romantics, three of whom survived into the 1890's. It follows that what we lacked in this country was not, certainly, a Romantic Movement, but a Victorian era at all comparable with England's. Our Victorianism was both brief and undistinguished.

And now the fourth and last main factor, *realism*— the application of the scientific spirit to art—reliance upon the senses and common sense, whether in their naïve working or in that organized working which Huxley describes. Although the scientific spirit gained a secure hold in the century of Benjamin Franklin, it did not really flourish in our literature till after the romantic dispensation. Realism, indeed, had been implicit in romanticism itself: keenness of sense perception, awareness of the complexities of the inner life, exploration of "the near, the low, the common," concern with "the poor, the feelings of the child, the philosophy of the street, the meaning of household life," in a word, "insight into today" as opposed to "the remote, the romantic,"—these "auspicious signs of the coming days" which Emerson discerned in 1837, in the full flush of romanticism, only needed emphasis in order to render possible the new literature that came to be known as realistic. To give this emphasis was, historically considered, the prime achievement of Walt Whitman. While he belonged to the romantics by virtue of his splendid personality, his doctrine of individualism and humanitarianism, and his religion of nature and the soul, he unmistakably points forward at the same time to the sophisticated realism of our time, by virtue of his sharp sense perception, his unflinching attitude toward facts of life shunned by what Edward Carpenter termed the "impure hush" of the Victorian era, his revolt from the modes of versification of the past and his experiment with the form now known as free verse. He anticipated our literature, also, in his attitude toward science, despite the mysticism that ever crowned his acceptance of science. Poetry is the child of science, "exuding the greatness of the father." From science he

derives authority for his treatment of sex: "The innocence and nakedness are resumed—they are neither
modest nor immodest." From science he derives the idea
of "vital laws" higher than those of the theology that
came out of the Orient: "The whole theory of the
supernatural, and all that was twined with it or educed
out of it, departs as in a dream." It is everywhere obvious that in science, whose standards underlie all modern realism, Whitman found, or believed that he found,
ample support for those aspects of his work which
repelled his contemporaries and which attract many
readers in our day of science in life and realism in the
arts.

I can only touch upon the subsequent development
of realism, the result partly of spontaneous reaction
against decadent romanticism, and partly of fresh European influence. Between 1870 and 1890, while such men
as Burroughs, Muir, and Fiske were demonstrating the
claims of science, and while the poets remained predominantly romantic, the cause of realism in literature
was advanced by such prose writers as Mark Twain,
Howells, James, Eggleston, Miss Murfree, Miss Jewett,
and Miss Wilkins (are these our "Eminent Victorians"?). In the revolt of the 1890's—in men like
Garland, Markham, and Crane—realism attained a bit-
terness that contrasts with the optimism of Whitman.
In Mr. Robinson and Mrs. Wharton it became more

rational and satirical and ironic; and at length came the "New Poetry," a poetry not without romantic elements, but distinguished in the main by its subtle sense observation, its rational and satiric outlook on life, and its eager experiment to find instruments of expression in keeping with the new vision. After 1916, when this poetry had reached its highest point, the realistic impulse centered in prose, in the short story, the novel, and the drama, giving special heed to the scientific contribution known as the "new psychology."

Such in brief is my own reading of the factors dominant in the evolution of American literature. Perhaps I have chosen them wrongly; that is not the question. The question is, whether we do not need, for our future historical studies and our criticism, a fresh interpretation of the forces that have directed our literature.

I need not detail our other needs, which are many. Our scholarship will attend, with exemplary patience, to the uncovering of new materials and facts. Professor Pollard, in his recent *Factors in American History,* confesses that he is not tempted "to add to the mass of excellent research which now pours out in such a volume from American historians that one wonders that even the United States can contain it all." Is it not true that American *literary* historians are already threatening to expand our knowledge beyond the power of controlling that knowledge? The danger that confronts the higher study of American literature is an aimless accumulation of small facts. Additions to the sum of knowledge are rarely of value unless they are related with an important end in view. No doubt we could go on forever building mountains of fact to the wonderment of Europeans like Professor Pollard; but our proper task is really to use the materials already at hand, and to seek new materials intelligently.

This cannot be done, I fear, on the basis of our antiquated interpretation of American literature. In order to work intelligently, we need a fresh interpretation, or a number of fresh interpretations—the systematic exploitation of promising points of view. Each possible main factor should be extensively applied to see how much it really explains. Different groups of students could work on different lines: some, for example, on the moral and religious background; some on the Revolutionary tradition; some on the manifold effects of the pioneer spirit; some on the Romantic Movement in America; and some on the realistic and scientific movement since Whitman. Each of these themes merits an extensive and thorough book; and until the books have been made possible by coöperative effort, I do not see how the state of American literary history can be measurably improved.

## III. THE FRONTIER

### JAY B. HUBBELL

I

THE frontier as a factor in American literature furnishes a striking example of the protracted neglect, by students of our literature, of methods and points of view that had been found revolutionary in the field of American history. In a memorable paper on "The Significance of the Frontier in American History," read in 1893 before the American Historical Association, Frederick J. Turner emphasized the importance of the frontier and outlined a program for the study of the field. Since that time the historians have worked the entire field so thoroughly that in 1924 Frederic L. Paxson could publish a *History of the American Frontier,* which seems almost final. Yet it was thirty years after the publication of Turner's paper before any one made a real application of his point of view to American literature. As one looks back now, one wonders why it was necessary to wait for Turner to show us the historical or the literary importance of the frontier. It is all implicit in Whitman's "Pioneers! O Pioneers!" and in Emerson's famous remark, "Europe extends to the Alleghanies; America lies beyond." Surely, in the field of American literature, we need not only a more exact but also a more imaginative scholarship.

Every discussion of the frontier must inevitably begin with Turner's epoch-making paper of 1893. The following extract makes clear his point of view:

The wilderness masters the colonist. It finds him a European in dress, industries, tools, modes of travel, and thought. It takes him from the railroad car and puts him in the birch canoe. It strips off the garments of civilization and arrays him in the hunting shirt and the moccasin. It puts him in the log cabin of the Cherokee and Iroquois and runs an Indian palisade around him. Before long he has gone to planting Indian corn and plowing with a sharp stick; he shouts the war cry and takes the scalp in orthodox Indian fashion. In short, at the frontier the environment is at first too strong for the man. He must accept the conditions which it furnishes, or perish, and so he fits himself into the Indian clearings and follows the Indian trails. Little by little he transforms the wilderness, but the outcome is not the old Europe, not simply the development of Germanic germs. . . . The fact is, that here is a new product that is American. . . . Thus the advance of the frontier has meant a steady movement away from the influence of Europe, a steady growth of independence on American lines. And to study this advance, the men who grew up under these conditions, and the political, economic, and social results of it, is to study the really American part of our history.[1]

By the term *frontier* the historians do not, of course, mean anything resembling the sharply defined and strongly fortified Franco-German border. The American frontier is (or was) the no man's land which separates civilization from savagery. In its widest sense the word has come to be used as almost identical with the geographic environment. It includes such factors as the immense and isolating distance which separates America from Europe—and, in turn, the Atlantic seaboard from the region west of the Appalachians; the absence of many European customs and institutions; the abundance of free land, which gave America an unparalleled economic opportunity; and the presence of many nationalities and many shades of opinion on the border. The frontier was a rapidly shifting, ever-changing thing; as it gradually receded westward, it continually took on new colors from the changing environment. It was less a definite area than a form of society or a complex of habits of thought, feeling, and action.

[1] Turner, *The Frontier in American History*, p. 4.

Among the historians there has been singularly little adverse criticism of Turner's point of view. A skeptic, distrustful of formulas, might ask whether the historians, in their interpretation of American history, have not leaned too heavily upon the economic and geographic factors. Is it not possible that the frontier influence has, in the main, merely accentuated tendencies already in operation in the Old World? For example, the world-wide growth of democracy during the past century would suggest that other influences have played an important part in that growth in this country as well as in Europe. England, always remote from the frontier, has apparently a better working democracy than our own. One might ask further whether the frontier in Latin America, Australia, and South Africa has exerted such an influence as it is supposed to have exerted in the United States? Such questions must of course be answered by the historians themselves. They are mentioned here merely to suggest that, if we push the frontier influence in American literature too far, we shall ultimately have to revise our interpretation in the light of later developments in American historical study. We cannot assume that the continued study of our history will lead to no new approaches or interpretations.

In applying Turner's point of view to American literature, we should also remember that history and literature are not interchangeable terms. If, as Turner believes, "The true point of view in the history of this nation is not the Atlantic coast; it is the Great West," does it necessarily follow that the true point of view in our literary history is the same? Perhaps it does, but one should remember that our literature has always been less American than our history; possibly it is not even yet a national literature in the full sense of the word. Our intellectual dependence upon Europe continued long after the political separation from the mother country—and still continues. In our cultural history foreign influences have been stronger than in our political and economic life. Although much of our political history was made on or near the frontier, our books have, as a rule, been written by authors, and for readers, quite remote from the frontier. American literature is, necessarily, a paler, less distinct reflection of the frontier than is our history.

There is yet another consideration to be borne in mind. Even those of our writers who have been most determined to employ only native materials have been dependent upon Europe for all that we call form or technique. Without Scott's novels, we should never have had the Leather-Stocking Tales, nor perhaps *The Scarlet Letter*. For *The Song of Hiawatha*, Longfellow borrowed the metrical form of the Finnish *Kalevala*. In

Taine's *Art of the Netherlands* Edward Eggleston found a suggestion for the method which he employed in *The Hoosier Schoolmaster*. Owen Wister's first Western story was, by his own admission, modeled on a story by Prosper Mérimée. And, if we may believe Conrad Aiken, our poets of today are as deeply indebted to Europe as to any of their predecessors. Amy Lowell, for example, probably owed as much to Europe as did her kinsman, James Russell Lowell.

## II

The frontier, as I see it, has made two distinct and important contributions to our literature: it has given our writers a vast field of new materials, and it has given them a new point of view, which we may call American.

Our early nineteenth century authors fell heir to a new and varied natural background, which appealed strongly to the Romantic imagination. Here they found the primeval forest, practically gone from Europe, and the great plains, not to be paralleled in Europe outside of Russia; they found rivers to which the Thames and the Tweed were pigmies, and mountains loftier than the Alps. Here was a new country, practically as large as the whole of Europe and rivaling Europe in its natural wonders and in its variety of climate and topography.

To the imagination of Romantic poets, America was almost Utopia come true; it was Nature (with a capital) comparatively uncorrupted by the defiling hand of man.

The American scene, too, was filled with new and striking character types. There was that romantic and mysterious child of Nature, the Indian, who enjoyed a vogue in the literatures of Europe before America had a literature. There was a whole tribe of frontier and semi-frontier types: the half-breed, the trader, the hunter, the trapper, the bush-ranger (*coureur-des-bois*), the scout, the missionary, the frontier soldier, the cowboy, the sheep-herder, the miner, the ranger, the gambler, the Pike, the "bad man," the "greaser," the squatter, the Mormon, the circuit-rider, the lumberjack, the Hoosier, the poor white, the Southern mountaineer, who lives in a curiously retarded frontier region; and we may perhaps include the varied types found in the Western oil fields of today. To these we must add the frontier women, less numerous but not less interesting than the men. All these frontier types were racy, individual, and quite distinct from European types. And their variety was greatly increased by the presence on the border of contrasting racial strains: Indian, English, Scotch-Irish, German, French, and Spanish.

It was in many respects a sordid and futile life which

the pioneers led, but it abounded in adventure, change, and freedom; and it was close to nature. On the border, truth was often stranger than the wildest of fiction. It is no wonder that our novelists have found in frontier life a wealth of incidents or that a few writers like Frank Norris have seen in the westward movement the last great epic event in history.

One must not forget, however, that the conquest of a great continent has not found expression adequate to its magnitude or importance. Cooper's Leather-Stocking Tales have a certain epic quality, but for too many of our writers the frontier has been a legend rather than a reality. Most of the novels that deal with the frontier were written by men who had had no first-hand experience of pioneer life. Consequently our frontier fiction is, as a rule, no "document" for the social historian; it represents a literary convention. Most of our major writers, living in metropolitan centers, had little opportunity to know frontier life; and the pioneers themselves were seldom writers, or even readers, of books. Socially, the frontier represents a primitive stage, an unliterary stage. Many other stages—not necessarily many years—had to follow before the descendants of the pioneers had any vital interest in describing the frontier and before the West had reached the economic and cultural level at which literature begins to be produced. Indeed, most parts of the West cannot be said even yet to have reached that level. It is not surprising, then, that many aspects of frontier life vanished before being accurately described; and now that the frontier is gone never to return, much of that life will probably never be adequately recorded. Few, except an occasional Hamlin Garland, care what the reality was. The popular novel, the cheap magazine, and the motion picture theater have commercialized the legend of the frontier; Zane Grey flourishes and Andy Adams is practically forgotten.

### III

The study of the frontier as subject matter is much less difficult than the accurate appraisal of the frontier influence in other directions. For here we deal with an influence which is indirect, protean, incessantly changing, interplaying with other factors almost equally elusive. The frontier influence in *The Last of the Mohicans* and "The Outcasts of Poker Flat" is easy to see, but what of the indirect frontier influence in Emerson's "The American Scholar" and Whitman's "Song of the Open Road"? Here we need to walk warily and to remember that this particular field has not yet been systematically studied. I merely suggest tentatively certain conclusions which I believe further investigation will warrant, and I do this primarily to suggest what lines our study should follow.

The frontier had an influence upon many of our writers who never saw it. The appeal of this vast Western hinterland to the imagination of those who lived upon the Atlantic seaboard is difficult to estimate, but it undoubtedly existed. If Henry James could explain the difference between Turgeniev and the typical French novelist by saying that the back door of the Russian's imagination was always open upon the endless Russian steppes, surely the existence of the American frontier helps to explain some of the differences between Emerson and Whitman and their British contemporaries, Carlyle and Tennyson. Hawthorne told Howells that he "would like to see some part of the country on which the . . . shadow of Europe had not fallen"; and even the domestic Longfellow longed to share Frémont's exhilarating experiences in the far West, although he sighed, "Ah, the discomforts!"

If our literature is a reflection of the national character, it should be strongly colored by our experience with the frontier. For it was chiefly the frontier influence which, as Norman Foerster has said, "transformed the European type into such men as Jefferson, Jackson, Lincoln, and Roosevelt, or, among the writers, Emerson, Whitman, and Mark Twain." Turner believes

THE FRONTIER

that the frontier supplies the key to the American character. "To the frontier," says he, "the American intellect owes its striking characteristics. That coarseness and strength combined with acuteness and inquisitiveness; that practical, inventive turn of mind, quick to find expedients; that masterful grasp of material things, lacking in the artistic but powerful to effect great ends; that restless, nervous energy; that dominant individualism, working for good and for evil, and withal that buoyancy and exuberance which comes with freedom—these are traits of the frontier, or traits called out elsewhere because of the existence of the frontier." [2]

To what extent are these frontier traits to be seen in our literature? Mr. Turner himself, in a letter to the writer, says, "I thoroughly agree that what is distinctive in American, in contrast to general English literature, comes out of our experience with the frontier, broadly considered." It is natural, I think, to conclude that there is, in the writings of such men as Whitman, Mark Twain, and William James, something distinctively American which comes indirectly from the frontier; but it is no easy matter to put one's finger upon it and say, Here it is. A good case can be made out for much of our political writing, which is closer to our life than most of what is known as *belles-lettres*.

[2] *The Frontier in American History*, p. 37.

Indeed, Bliss Perry finds that the dominant note in American literature is the civic note, which surely owes much to frontier democracy. Dr. Canby has argued, too, that the "nature book," perhaps the only new literary type which America has given the world, grew out of our fathers' experience with the frontier and our own longing for the vanished frontier environment.

Much of what we are accustomed to call American literature, however, has no discernible connection with the frontier; the work of Edgar Allan Poe is a conspicuous example. Much of our literature is un-American, imitative of Europe. Too often, as John Macy has pointed out, it is distinguished by just those qualities which the American intellect is supposed to lack: it is dainty, polished, fanciful, sentimental, feminine, and "literary." The contemporary revolt against our cis-Atlantic Victorians, however, would indicate that many of our older writers were out of harmony with what now seems to be the genuine American tradition.

American literature has become a national literature—if we may now call it national—largely through what Van Wyck Brooks, in a letter to the writer, has called "the sublimation of the frontier spirit." American literature has become increasingly American. It may be well here to try to indicate the part which the frontier has played in the nationalization of our literature.

The American Revolution, the historians tell us, was in large measure due to the political and economic influence of the frontier. In the new environment had grown up a people to whom the English were comparative strangers. Under the stress of the common struggle, first against France and later against England, a new national consciousness had developed in the thirteen colonies, which finally declared themselves a new nation. The frontier conception of democracy, modified of course by European political theory and experience, was written into the Declaration of Independence. Eventually it brought about something akin to a social and economic revolution in American life.

With the achievement of political independence and with the natural reaction against all things English, it was inevitable that there should arise a demand for a national literature which should express the new national culture. It was felt that a nation whose political and social life was based on democratic principles should have a literature quite unlike that of undemocratic Britain. A good deal of ignorance of literary history and a certain lack of logic are seen in the reasoning of the advocates of a national literature; and the literature which they prophesied was not born full-grown like Minerva from the brain of Jove. Nevertheless from the early nineteenth century down to the present there has been a succession of declarations of cultural and intellectual independence from England. These include Emerson's "The American Scholar," Whitman's Preface to *Leaves of Grass*, Mark Twain's *Innocents Abroad*, and Van Wyck Brooks's *America's Coming of Age*. The new national literature, however, did not come in response to the immediate demand. It was the Romantic Movement, and not the outmoded neo-classical literary tradition, which gave American writers the technical methods of putting the national life into literature. Ultimately, however, as Carl Van Doren has pointed out, the Revolution became one of the "three matters of American romance," the other two being the Settlement and the Frontier. (All three "matters," in fact, derive from the frontier.)

Perhaps the influence of Jacksonian democracy had something to do with Whitman's attempt to create a native American literature. Whitman of course was not a frontiersman, but there is a certain analogy between what he and the Jacksonian democrats tried to accomplish. Emerson was too much the scholar and the gentleman to attempt all that Whitman tried to do, but he saw hope even in the Jacksonians for the future of American literature. Lamenting the cultural dependence of America upon England, he wrote in his Journal in 1834: "I suppose the evil may be cured by this rank

rabble party, the Jacksonism of the country, heedless
of English and all literature—a stone cut out of the
ground without hands;—they may root out the hollow
dilettantism of our cultivation in the coarsest way, and
the newborn may begin again to frame their own world
with greater advantage."

The Civil War gave a great impetus to national tendencies in all fields and did much to complete the work
left incomplete by the Revolution. It brought about
"the birth of a nation," and in literature it led to what
Fred Lewis Pattee has called "the second discovery of
America." By abolishing slavery and settling the question of secession, the War made the nation a political
unit that it had never been before. Americans gradually
ceased to say, "The United States *are*," and began to
say, "The United States *is*." Political and military leadership passed from New England and the South to the
more thoroughly American Middle West, which, in
Lowell's phrase, gave us "the first American," Abraham
Lincoln. The Civil War stimulated the progress of the
economic or industrial revolution, which, more than
any other influence beside the frontier, has made the
whole country an economic and cultural unit. In ante-
bellum days American literature was little more than
an aggregation of sectional literatures; after the War it

became national in a sense of the word not applicable before that time.

In the Americanization of our literature the West, especially the Middle West, played a leading part. The writings of New Englanders and New Yorkers did not satisfy the West. Edward Eggleston, jealous of the literary domination of New England, wrote *The Hoosier Schoolmaster* to show that Indiana furnished as rich materials for the novelist as Massachusetts. Bret Harte and other young men, so he tells us, were trying to create a California literature. A more important spokesman for the West was Mark Twain. What Ibsen and Tolstoy were to nineteenth century Europe, that or something like it Mark Twain was to the United States: a new region had found a spokesman, and what he had to say did not resemble the work of Hawthorne and Longfellow. A new spirit also began to move the reconstructed and reviving South; and the more cosmopolitan spirit of the Middle Atlantic states blended with the influence of the South and the West to create something approximating a national point of view in our literature.

Meanwhile the best work of nearly all the great New Englanders had been done. The Romantic impulse had become conventional, and the influence of European realism was becoming apparent. Upon Howells, a Westerner by birth, had descended the editorial mantle of the *Atlantic Monthly.* But Howells was thoroughly de-Westernized, and New England assimilated him without great difficulty. It was to his friend Mark Twain that New England objected as representing the Western barbarians of literature. At the Whittier birthday dinner of the *Atlantic* in 1877, the custodians of the Brahmin tradition condemned in no uncertain manner the vulgarity of the literary West. Howells tells us that of the Boston-Cambridge group only Francis James Child and Charles Eliot Norton made anything of the man whom Howells regarded as "the Lincoln of our literature"; even Lowell did not warm to him. The current of events, however, was too strong for the Brahmins. Howells himself went to New York, thereby admitting that the literary scepter had passed from Boston. New York is now our publishing center, our literary capital, if we have one; but the productive center of American literature is perhaps nearer Chicago. Certainly the Middle West aspires to cultural as well as industrial leadership, and it is significant that the favorite background of contemporary fiction is the Middle West.

IV

One must not, as I have said, push the frontier influence too far. Our literary history is the result of the interplay of complex and changing influences, political, economic, social, cultural, educational—sectional, national, foreign. Properly to understand and appraise the influence of the frontier, one must thoroughly understand all the other influences and their interrelations. It is just here, it seems to me, that Mrs. Hazard's *The Frontier in American Literature* conspicuously fails.

The frontier influence is not the only influence making for nationalism in American literature. At least two other historical factors have had a part in it. In the first place, the immigrants who came to this country from the very beginning did not represent the English type in race, in religious beliefs, or in social status. They were, to a large extent, nonconformists; nor were these by any means confined to New England, as we too often suppose. The nonconformists played a large part in the development of the American bourgeoisie, with its well-known attitude toward art and literature. Immigration, moreover, was itself a selective process. The more restless and the more aggressive came, whereas the conservative, as a rule, remained in Europe. The character of our immigrants accounts in part for the peculiar American blend of radicalism and conservatism which strikes our foreign critics as odd. Many of the immigrants, however, even in Colonial times, were not

English or even British. Mr. Mencken and Professor Schlesinger have argued that the fine arts in America have been developed largely by men of mixed blood. At any rate, the typical American would not be a typical Englishman even had there been no influence from the frontier.

Another influence making for nationalism is the economic or industrial revolution. In the course of a century American life has become predominantly urban; and it is based very largely upon machinery. As a result, American life is to a great degree uniform throughout the country. The same tendency toward standardization is found in our books, our magazines, and our schools. Even those who rebel against the tyrannous uniformity of American life and thought seem to rebel *en masse,* as it were, and merely substitute the conventions of the *American Mercury* for those of the *Saturday Evening Post*—as if one could by any such change of front become individual and original.

In our eagerness to point out the national tendencies in our literature, one should not overlook the sectional. Most of those engaged in research in American literature have been prejudiced against the sectional approach by the poor quality of existing sectional studies. Even the political historians have neglected sectional tendencies, except as they concern the slavery issue, so much that Turner has felt it necessary in a recent article [3] to urge a new study of sectionalism in American history. The frontier influence, in the main a national one, has at times made for sectionalism. In Colonial times it was the frontier which created the first sectionalism of West against East. In our own day we have seen the semi-frontier West, sometimes allied with the South, arrayed against the industrial belt of North and East.

To understand the literary influence of the frontier, one must study it in connection with the influences which came from Europe. Influences from abroad have increased rather than diminished, for the revolution in methods of transportation and communication has brought Europe closer to New York than Boston and Philadelphia were a century ago. European literary fashions have to a large extent determined the manner in which our writers have portrayed the pioneers.

V

Before bringing this essay to a conclusion, it seems necessary to insist that, if our literary historians are to continue to use the term *frontier*, it must be carefully defined. To a layman, it would seem that even the historians sometimes use the term loosely. "In the census reports," says Turner, "it is treated as the margin of

[3] *Op. cit.*, p. 7, note.

that settlement which has a density of two or more to the square mile. The term is an elastic one, and for our purposes does not need sharp definition. We shall consider the whole frontier belt, including the Indian country and the outer margin of the 'settled area' of the census reports." [4] In justice to Turner, it should be stated that he was, in his own words, attempting only "to call attention to the frontier as a fertile field for investigation, and to suggest some of the problems which arise in connection with it." [5] Professor Paxson notes that "The American frontier was a line, a region, or a process, according to the context in which the word is used," [6] but even he attempts no exact definition of the term.

Careful historians like Paxson and Turner doubtless have a fairly definite meaning in mind even though they do not take the trouble of defining the word. Many persons without the scholar's feeling for accuracy use the term very loosely. The word has acquired certain connotations which do not properly belong to it. It has a poetic flavor; it suggests something native, something fine and romantic which other countries conspicuously lack. But to one who has read Hamsun's *Growth of the Soil,* the opening pages of Butler's *Erewhon,* or the

[4] *The Frontier in American History,* p. 3.
[5] *Ibid.*
[6] *A History of the American Frontier,* p. 43.

*Oxford Book of Australasian Verse,* it is permissible to doubt whether the American frontier is quite unique. We are in danger of forgetting the sordid side of the American frontier. Among Westerners in particular the term has much the same glamor that the *Old South* has in Virginia or the *Pilgrim Fathers* in New England. There is a halo about the forehead of the pioneer. Such provincial pride, amounting sometimes to ancestor worship, inevitably interferes with the historian's seeing things as they are. After all, are the economic and geographic influences implied in the term frontier essentially different from those to be found in sparsely settled regions the world over?

Our literary historians have used the word *frontier* more loosely than the historians; the term has become increasingly vague and ambiguous. Like the *Celtic spirit,* the *Greek influence, Romanticism, Classicism,* and *Realism,* the term *frontier* may be made to mean whatever the user wishes it to mean. The frontier should not be identified with all the national influences in our literature; it should not be identified with the geographic environment. The frontier passes; the natural background remains, often unchanged. The Adirondacks and the Marshes of Glynn once belonged to the frontier, but not today.

In literature there are two fairly definite uses of the

word which seem legitimate. We may properly refer to the frontier as a literary background. There is no ambiguity here except when we include semi-frontier regions, as we often do. We may also use the word when we refer to the beginnings of literary activity on the frontier, as in Professor Rusk's *The Literature of the Middle Western Frontier.*

A third common use of the term, however, calls for closer definition. We have too often identified the frontier with *all* the national influences in our literary history. The sources of the national spirit are, as I have tried to indicate, more numerous; and the whole problem is quite complex. If we do not use the term more carefully, we shall soon find it as thoroughly discredited as Taine's famous formula. I do not think we can dispense with the term, but I do expect that we shall use it more accurately. If we do not, the results of our investigation may be no more creditable to American scholarship than are the works of certain of our predecessors whom we need not name here.

## IV. THE EUROPEAN BACKGROUND

### HOWARD MUMFORD JONES

A MERICAN literature belongs to the great family of west-European literatures. In so far as it differs from other members of the group, it has become distinctively American. In studying the national letters these are, I take it, the two primary elements in the problem.

To the Americanism of American literature a vast deal of labor has been devoted. Historians have traced sympathetically the struggles of native genius to throw off European modes or to adapt the conventions of British letters to the American theme. Indeed, writers have so frequently envisioned the European background as inherently hostile to native genius that they are prone to exalt any attribute that makes for specific "Americanism" with little regard to its esthetic value; and to depreciate or ignore (as in the case of Mark Twain or Howells or Garland) other qualities that link the American with Europe.

But such a presentation of the story of our literature is merely mystical. Its very assumptions are faulty. It assumes that American literature develops under the guidance of providence. It assumes that the figurative seeds planted by Captain John Smith and the Pilgrim fathers had some mysterious power of germination and growth until by slow degrees the tree of literature reared its stately head. One would think from reading the usual textbook that Puritanism was something unique in the history of mankind; that, the *Mayflower* once arrived, the development of New England culture happened in a kind of vacuum. And because these writers assume the law of "progress," they are compelled to write as if the New England divines must of necessity have been followed by the political literature of the eighteenth century, and this in turn by the Hartford wits, the Knickerbocker group, and what not, until transcendentalism and Poe and the realistic novel and contemporary poetry arrive in due course. But there is nothing in seventeenth century American literature to prophesy that American letters should take just this shape; and the intellectual progress from the Mathers to Brown, and from Brown to Poe, from Poe to Whitman, from Whitman to Cabell, is not progress, it is a series of amazing jerks. There is no cause-and-effect relationship—sometimes no relationship at all; nor is the assumption of that relationship any more valid when we add the economic and social factors of American civilization. American letters cannot be wholly "explained" either by reference to themselves or by reference to American history. Something is lacking. That something is a constant reference to the cultural fact that America is part of the west-European world.

Here I would not be misunderstood. I am aware that every student knows that Washington Irving followed the *Spectator* tradition; that Emerson and Poe were variously conscious of German romanticism; that Hamlin Garland read Taine and William Dean Howells read Turgeniev. I am aware that specific problems of sources have been dealt with individually. American opinion of English, German, French, and Spanish letters has been haphazardly traced. But none of these things gets at the root of the matter.

Unless American letters are seen in their comparative relationship I do not see how their real meaning and importance can be grasped; and far from believing that such a study will further belittle their dignity, I am of the opinion that it is the approach which will reveal their extraordinary significance in the pattern of western thought. We must see that American literature is not merely a thing in itself, but a part of the intellectual history of the cultural unit to which we inevitably belong. Professors of the subject seem to be suffering from an inferiority complex; conscious that they have to present no Shakespeare or Goethe or Dante, they have developed a morbid fear that comparisons prove them odious. But the fear destroys the very thing they are after; namely, the establishing of the significance of American letters.

References to European writers in histories of American literature are accordingly naïve. When, for example, these books reach the Revolutionary Epoch, they make some random reference to Locke and Montesquieu and Burke and Pitt, but that is all; there is no comprehension of the relationship among all the west-European literatures in the eighteenth century. And, the Revolution once past, though the reader may learn that American magazines patterned after British reviews or that Bryant is a "chilly Wordsworth," he will never dream that American letters in the Napoleonic era, and after, partook of the same reactionary tendency which runs from the Scandinavias to Italy and from Russia to the Mississippi. Of the New England group it is conventional to make some reference to Carlyle and the Germans, but the understanding is not deep; and as for that curious current of western thought which characterizes the second Revolutionary Epoch (1830-1848), the student will never suspect that the movement of American thought is one with the movement of European thought—that movement curiously compounded of spiritual exaltation, a belief in vast, vague phrases, a canorous political and social phraseology, the exaltation of machinery and industry, and a naïve faith in science, which makes the second quarter of the nineteenth century so amusing and so amazing. But why go on? There is clearly something wrong with the picture.

But, before proceeding, it may be well to be clear. I am not saying we should abandon everything for the comparative method. We may well continue to expose college students to survey courses in the American field in the interests of filling their vacuum tanks with a stock of socially acceptable phrases. We may, and should, begin establishing correct texts for many literary documents: no field of scholarship is poorer in scientific text-making. Most of the biographies need to be revised. We should encourage the study of regional movements in our letters. And I do not deny that there are certain attitudes, certain ideas in literature which make it "American," though I confess that when I come to delimit these ideas and attitudes from the ideas and attitudes of the western world generally, I am often at a loss to see the difference; and I hesitatingly advance the hypothesis that the difference between Americanism and Europeanism, if there is any, is mainly a difference in rhythm and tempo, supposing these terms to have meaning. But the main value of this branch of research generally, aside from a few great men who ascend to the plane where esthetic appreciation is profitable, seems to me to lie in the light it throws upon the nature, the sources, and the probable future of American culture. It is when we come to this point that we are peculiarly in need of the comparative method.

For example, seventeenth century American literature is sadly misjudged. It is mainly theological, it is true; yet in the midst of these polemics we see emerging here and there apologies for the natural man. In sum, Merrymount and Jonathan Edwards' study are the two poles between which it oscillates. Now the obvious parallel with British literature has not been neglected, and it is commonly said that Puritan and Cavalier attitudes were transplanted to the New World, and there the matter ends. But does it? The two grand struggles of seventeenth century thought seem to me to be, on the one hand, the debate over the theological man as opposed to the natural man—between human nature according to Calvin and human nature according to Rabelais. And on the other hand there is the titanic struggle between humanism and science; that is to say, the struggle of the successors of Erasmus to maintain their supremacy against the attacks of men like Bacon and Descartes. Should man devote himself to the glory of God or to the study of nature? And if nature be the creation of God, and man a part of it, should he trust to his endowments and his instincts, or flee in terror from the wickedness of the world to the grace mysteriously vouchsafed him by the God of Loyola or the God of Luther? Something like this was the problem with which all the mighty intellects of the period had to grapple. It convulsed the fine spirit of Pascal as it drove Bunyan past Apollyon to the Celestial City. It produced the magnificent apologia of *Paradise Lost* and the grim tragedy of *Samson Agonistes*, just as it lent meaning to the profound psychology of Racine and La Rochefoucauld, and created the splendor and pity of Bossuet. This it was that drove Rochester to cynicism and John Dryden to the Catholic church. It was the central problem of western culture; and it is idle to suppose that the Europeans transplanted, half-unwillingly, to the New World, were blind to the conflict. On the contrary they faced it boldly; they participated in it; they bought European books to inform themselves of the issues, and themselves contributed their quota of literature and science to the battle. Viewed thus, the innumerable tracts and pamphlets of the Pilgrim fathers, the reports of gentlemen amateurs on the flora and fauna of the New World, the struggles of divines to achieve and maintain spiritual stability for themselves and their flocks, are no longer the petty squabbles of theological zealots nor the miraculous beginnings of a providentially inspired literature; they are a chapter in the vast volume of seventeenth century controversy, and belong to the same generation as Milton and Racine and Glanvill and Spinoza and Leibnitz.

The principle of authority having been broken down in the theological and metaphysical worlds, the conflict was next transferred to the world of action; and the eighteenth century witnessed its great political struggles. But the parallel of revolutionary thought in America and in Europe is too obvious to require comment; so obvious, indeed, as to have induced much futile source-hunting for the genesis of American political theory—futile, because it is not specific verbal indebtedness but the generation of a particular intellectual atmosphere that is here important. What has been ignored, however, is that in the western world, after the demolition of old systems of thought, there followed attempts to construct new ones on a positive basis: whence the grandiose system-mongering of the period from Hobbes to Sieyès. Locke, Diderot, Condillac, Helvétius, Rousseau, Godwin, Herder, each in turn tries to rebuild the universe, sometimes by a constitution, sometimes by a philosophy. What is the American Constitution but such a rebuilding, what are the democratic and scientific theories of Jefferson but such a reconstruction? The question of the specific indebtedness of Madison to Montesquieu is of less importance than the contribution of this new nation, this latest extension of Europe, to contemporary knowledge in the shape of an actual experiment. And the creation of the United States did not separate the new republic from monarchical Europe; on the contrary it drew the two continents closer together; and the correspondence back and forth, the feverish publication of reports in the Old World about the experiment in the New, the repercussion of these documents in the United States, are all testimony to the fact that intellectually Europe and the United States are one.

But something of this has been grasped even by the historians of American letters. It is when they get beyond the Constitution that they go wildly astray. No period of our letters is more unsatisfactorily "organized" than the stretch between the publication of *The Federalist* and the emergence of New England Transcendentalism. I think this has been true because the principle of its organization has not been grasped. It was the period of the conservative reaction.

In Europe the French Revolution became the Napoleonic world, and this in turn became the system of Metternich. With the imprisonment of the Scourge of God men drew a long breath and resolved that Europe should not be disturbed again. In every department of life there was a movement back to authority. In France young Lamartine and Hugo hymned the throne and the altar and Comte du Maistre argued brilliantly in *Du Pape* for absolutism in church and state. In Germany the Schlegels led the way to medievalism in art and Catholicism in theology. In England Wordsworth and Coleridge became the apologists of things as they were, Burke formed every gentleman's mind, and Byron and Shelley were cast out. The faint promise of Italian literature in Gozzi and Goldoni and Casti became the political turncoatism of Monti. Leopardi took refuge in classical archeology, and Landor in imaginary conversations. In Russia Pushkin was politely muzzled and Turgeniev went into exile. And with this checking of the movement of literature there came a religio-moral revival. Then occurred a great neo-Catholic movement. Mysticism and even magic were fashionable, and there was a deal of circumambient hocus-pocus. The Oxford Movement is the culmination of an English religious revival, and in the empire of the czars the doctrine of Holy Russia was invented. Meanwhile art, because it could not deal with political, philosophical, and social ideas held to be disturbing, took refuge in "mere" beauty, in moralizing, in a return to the past. Keats, Wackenroder, Novalis, de Nerval, Hoffmann, Tennyson in his younger days are evidence of the first movement. The novel, which in the hands of Rousseau, Godwin, Tieck, Voltaire, and Goethe had been the vehicle of ideas, and which became the purveyor of a blameless didacticism, as written by Mme. de Genlis and Hannah More, is evidence of the second movement. And the historical novel which fell into more powerful hands— since creative energy was freest to deal with periods that could not disturb the present—the historical novel of Scott, de Vigny, young Balzac, and Bulwer Lytton in his earlier stages, is evidence for the third movement. A vast silence fell upon literature, broken only by the mutterings of Alfred de Musset in the great opening chapters of *The Confessions of a Child of the Century.*

With a change of names does not this read curiously like the history of American letters from 1793 to the publication of *Nature* in 1836? The novel became historical, exploiting the colonial and revolutionary past. Dwight, Barlow, Alsop, Humphreys, Washington Irving, Paulding became the apologists of things as they were. Poe was writing the poetry of "mere" beauty. The magazines developed an enormous didactic literature, hortatory, conservative, uninspired. Bryant was of the opinion that God is in his heaven, and all's death in the world. A vast religious revival swept over the country, crushing out deism in the South and West and establishing colleges and academies to hold the ebullient frontier in check. The ideas of the French Revolution were viewed with horror and the experimental literature of romanticism with distrust. Men watched with anxious eyes the development of European theology and philosophy: of neo-Calvinism in Geneva, of liberal Christianity in Paris and ultra-montanism in Rome, of Puseyism at Oxford, of transcendentalism in Germany and eclecticism at the Sorbonne. All over the western world the triumphant bourgeoisie were in power; the bankers and the peerage ruled; and in America industry, invention, and commerce were hymned in the reviews and praised in the pulpits.

But the reaction could not last, and movements of revolutionary significance again appeared—transcendentalism and unitarianism in New England, romanticism in France, the movements of young Germany and young Italy, even a young America movement. Men took up once more their glamorous phrases about democracy and constitutionalism. There was abolitionism at home, and chartism and communism abroad. A thousand panaceas for social ills appeared, a thousand paper utopias were drafted. Men died on the barricades for vague phrases which the writers furnished them; and if there were no barricades in Washington, there were cleavage between North and South, bitter conflicts in religion, and the same vague belief in optimism, progress, and manifest destiny which informs the work of Mazzini and Mrs. Browning and Hugo and Heine—sometimes. Conservative Britons, viewing the American experiment, reported unfavorably and were hotly rebuked in American journals; liberal Germans went to the United States as to the promised land. Are we to believe that these struggles were viewed with indifference or neglected by Americans? That American literature is as remote from Europe as if it had been produced in Alaska? The textbooks seem to think so.

But where, it may be asked, is the evidence for any such reciprocal intellectual commerce? Professor Faÿ and Professor Chinard have shown us. The evidence is so obvious that it has been overlooked. The correspondence, the diaries, the journals, and above all the magazines and newspapers of the time simply overflow with excited comments on Europe, on America, on the march of the human mind. But writers, committed to a chauvinistic attitude, have ignored these things because there was no evidence of verbal indebtedness, because they must show above all the Americanism of American literature, and a whole important segment of the field has been boarded off and neglected. But we must abandon this provincialism; we must group Europe and the United States into the homogeneous unity of western culture; and seek to determine by comparison the differences and likenesses between them.

American literature is none the less American; and if we are part of Europe, we have not accepted everything European, we have repelled certain portions of European culture and accepted other portions. The search for the factors which make American literature individual is again concerning us, and much good spade work has been done. Investigators, yielding to a commendable enthusiasm, have unfortunately committed themselves to a policy of oversimplification, and a variety of diagnoses is available as to why American letters are American. Indeed, I have sinned in the direction of too much simplification myself. Some are for Puritanism, romanticism, and the frontier; some are for liberalism and conservatism; and some, abandoning all else, read everything from John Smith to Henry James in terms of the frontier. This surely is to abandon all critical judgment.

But whatever the factors may prove to be, they are complex; no single analysis can be satisfactory. I shall, however, venture to suggest one or two considerations which seem to me to have been thus far overlooked, and to indicate how helpful the comparative method may prove, not only to discover likenesses, but to sharpen differences as well.

The relation of American religion to our letters has

(except in the seventeenth century) been singularly neglected, and here again we must remember Europe. Indeed, most readers will view the phrase "American religion" with surprise. Producing scholars in the United States are too close to their environment to see how peculiar is the religious situation in America; they accept conditions too naturally to appreciate the profound significance of the American church in the history of culture. Yet, as the Roman Catholic church was the custodian of knowledge during the Middle Ages, so the American Protestant churches (because the Roman Catholics were in the minority) have been the nurse and mother of our culture. Not only did they nourish the early colleges in the East, but they strewed the Middle West and South with educational institutions intended to save the souls of the faithful from the heresies of Tom Paine and the wiles of the Scarlet Woman, and even yet their hand is heavy upon American education. Such colleges and academies were the foci of cultural life from Massachusetts to California. What they taught, or rather what the churches permitted them to teach, shaped the minds of generations of writers and readers; and, what is quite as significant, that which they disapproved was not taught. They have dominated endowed institutions directly, and tax-supported institutions indirectly; they have brought to education a consecration of energy wholly admirable, but they have brought little critical sense to higher education, and their fear of certain aspects of European thought has acted as a sieve to separate foreign orthodoxy from foreign heterodoxy.

Thus it is that the moral idealism of the Romantic Movement came in, and the moral anarchy of that movement was kept out, so that we have no American Shelley, no Godwin, no Gautier, no Heine and no Schopenhauer to deny conventional values, but in place of these, Emerson and Longfellow and Bryant and Lowell and Hawthorne, who have their merits doubtless, but who are not quite of the company of Nietzsche. Thus it is that the American "Romantic Movement" is a very correct romantic movement, one that has no *Lucinde,* no *Mademoiselle de Maupin,* in short, no passionate apology for the senses, just as it has no *Préface du Cromwell* and no first night of *Hernani,* but merely a riot over opera prices. How could it have been otherwise? American educational institutions, dominated by the American church, had no place for esthetics in their scheme of things, and no belief in art, and for that matter, they have little today. Yet it is only by comparing the life in European and American intellectual centers that we see how important it is to study the formative school years of writers; it is only when we remember how much philosophical, political, and artistic radicalism was nourished in certain European student groups, and how little in American colleges— it is only when we trace these differences to their sources in both cases that we see how the comparative method illumines the issue.

But it is not alone in education that the American church is one of the most important factors in American life. Its theology and doctrine shaped men's minds. An insistent individualism is its dominant note; conversion (an intensely personal experience) is the method; and an intimate relation of the single soul to God is the aim. Is this not poles removed from Catholicism—the Catholicism which helped to form Spanish and French and Italian and German writers to some degree? The attitudes preached in a myriad pulpits carried over into practical life; it was the doctrine of individualism, it was the doctrine of the earnestness of life and its radiant success at the end. Here was no pessimism, no dubiety, no mass movement, no institutionalism. And therefore it is that American readers agreed that Whittier was a great poet because he was very much in earnest, and Longfellow a profound moralist because he was a resigned and pious Christian. That is why readers cried up Emerson without understanding him and ignored Thoreau because they could not comprehend an individualism more subtle than their own;

why Howells and Garland and Hearne struggled long
to gain a hearing for a realism that was an old story on
the Continent; why the vague, benevolent optimism of
Lyman Beecher and Harriet Beecher Stowe and Unitarianism generally could thrill multitudes. And what
these pulpits failed to teach is equally primary. That
was a sense of social obligation. Their blankness in the
realm of business ethics explains the ruthless exploitation of natural resources in this country; this was the
promised land and we were the Hebrews. And what
the eighteenth century began, the nineteenth century
continued, and the twentieth century tardily repents.
When now we ask why the keen insight of men as
different as Whitman or Lowell not only failed to per-
ceive the wrong, but sometimes gloried in the process
of exploitation; why, when European authors had for
some decades been struggling with the social problem,
American authors were still belatedly weighing moral
problems, like Holmes, or bewailing bad politics in terms
of sin and conscience, like Curtis, we are led back once
more to the American church.

This is not all the story of course, but in view of
such obvious considerations it would seem that a careful study of American church history is one of the prime
requisites for the historian of American letters. It will
scarcely be believed by one ignorant of the field that no

such study has ever been made. To this day there exists not a single work to which a student can turn for an adequate understanding of American religious life. Church history has been either sectarian and far from accurate or profound; or non-sectarian, hesitating, and superficial. Timidity has prevented non-religious historians from speaking, and even important works like *The Chronicles of America* series, the *American Nation* series, and *The Cambridge History of American Literature* devote ten times the space to politics that they devote to religion. But this must change; the dust must be blown from these forgotten sermons, these bitter controversial pamphlets at ease in oblivion; theological issues must be re-studied by historians, and the profound effect of the American religion upon cultural life must be scrutinized. But it will not be sufficient to confine this study to the national church. The student will find that the genesis of American religious beliefs is European. He will find a continuing relation between European theological controversy and American theological controversy, between American Catholicism and European Catholicism. He will find that even when American politicians turned their backs on the Old World, American theologians did not. And he will find, lastly, that he can not understand the American religious system until he has compared it with the re-

ligious systems of Europe so that the differences between the two will sharpen his sense of what is distinctive in the American church.

Were there space, I should like to comment upon
the peculiar quality of so much of American literature
as is concerned with politics, as compared with the
quality of European literature of the same order, and
to show how in the one a legalistic and pragmatic note
is characteristic and in the other a metaphysical and
positive quality, for here, too, comparison will sharpen
our sense of what is "American." I should like also to
indicate how the growth of what Spengler calls the
megalopolitan areas in the United States has made for
cosmopolitan influences upon letters, and how, in Wal-
ter Lippman's phrase, the conflict between the village
and the city is one of the important conflicts in our
culture. It is the village which admires Longfellow,
Holmes, Riley, Julia Ward Howe, and Whittier; it is
the city which prefers Whitman, Cabell, Henry James,
Aldrich, Huneker, and Mencken. And it is obvious that
the second group of writers is more definitely in relation to European thought than is the first. But I have
done enough if I have called attention to the values for
the study of our letters which lie in the comparative
method, properly understood, a method which makes
American literature neither more nor less "American,"

neither more nor less important, a method which is more than hunting sources abroad for authors at home, a method which puts our literature in proper perspective and gives it a dignified and proper place in the march of the western mind.

# V. THE PURITAN TRADITION IN AMERICAN LITERATURE [1]

## KENNETH B. MURDOCK

THAT there is a Puritan tradition in American literature seems to be taken for granted. What it is, how it has manifested itself, and how and where it persists, are queries left unanswered or answered so variously as to breed new problems. Puritan baiters and ancestor worshipers alike take shelter in the mists of the undefined, and score easy victories in proving the existence of a baneful or beneficent Puritan literary tradition by nimbly avoiding the crux of the matter, the nature of Puritanism in so far as it affected literature. By Mr. Mencken many who disagree with him are airily disposed of as Puritans; to Mr. Brooks a middle class emphasis on material success and a contempt for the esthetic and for the larger pagan virtues are characteristic of Puritanism. The fundamentalist is called a Puritan, but so, now and then, are liberal innovators

[1] This paper was first presented, in substance, as a lecture (1927) at the Bread Loaf School of English, Bread Loaf, Vermont, the directors of which have approved its publication here.

in religious thought. Prohibition, by those who condemn it, is glibly named Puritanism, though there must be ironical laughter from the shades of the men who provided for wine and beer in what they thought was the Commonwealth of God. A law passed in 1890 is so construed in 1927 by two public officials in Boston as to make it necessary for their townsmen to order certain modern books from New York, and at once Boston becomes notorious as the last stronghold of Puritanism. A morbid interest in the physical aspects of sex is said by a modern historian to be "one of the most curious elements in the psychology of the Puritans," [2] though by others the same curiosity expressed in recent literature is hailed as a welcome revolt against the shackles of Puritan prudishness. We hear of the Puritans as reactionaries, and yet are told that much of our liberalism is the fruit of Puritan seed.[3] Nor is the case made clearer if the definition of Puritan influence is sought in the lives of individuals who are said to be under its spell. Hawthorne is a Puritan, and Emerson, we are told; but

[2] J. T. Adams, *The Founding of New England*, 1921, p. 265, note.

[3] Ludwig Lewisohn in "Un-Americanized Americans" (*Independent*, Vol. CXII, Nos. 173 and 178), speaks of American liberals with faith in the individual's right to freedom, asserting that "they all bear New England names . . . they all have in their veins the direct blood of the Transcendentalists and Abolitionists"—which is to say, of course, the blood of the Puritans—and assures us that from New Englanders and their descendants "the great protests, the great re-affirmations of what it means to be an American, have always come."

so is Andrews Norton, so is Longfellow, so are Calvin
Coolidge and Mr. Mencken, Wayne Wheeler and William James, Dr. Fosdick and Dr. Straton—all are herded
into the same stockade.

Indeed, one reason for the constant use of the epi-
thets Puritan and Puritanism is their very haziness. Any
term vague enough to include Cotton Mather and the
Babbitts of the moment has a usefulness denied to the
more explicit. As John Foster put it, Puritanism has
meant "any thing, every thing, which the vain world
disliked in the devout and conscientious character. To
the more sluggish it saved, and to the more loquacious
it relieved, the labor of endlessly repeating 'demure
rogues,' 'sanctimonious pretenders,' 'formal hypo-
crites.' " [4] A good deal is summed up in the shrewd comments of a Bostonian not unnaturally confused by the
variant winds of doctrine, who wrote: "The case against
the Puritans is conclusive. We of the present generation
have two kinds of faults; puritanical and otherwise—especially otherwise. The former are clearly a direct in-
heritance from the Puritans, the latter a reaction against
them. Both kinds are thus the faults of the Puritans and
of no one else. We ourselves, accordingly, have no faults.
This is what we have always felt, but it has never been
so clearly proved before. . . . For instance, if there is

[4] *Essays*, Andover, 1826, p. III.

nowadays too much divorce it is . . . due to the Puritan notion of having only one wife living at a time. . . . The divorcées are simply trying to redress the balance. . . . Our pedantry and illiteracy alike are obviously the Puritans' fault for founding public schools, and if America now burns negroes at the stake it is because the Puritans did not, like other Christian nations, burn their witches." [5]

The Puritan tradition in literature can mean nothing else than a tradition inspired and fostered by Puritans, and so long as Puritanism connotes different things to different writers and readers, the tradition must take its hue from the eyes which regard it. If I were to confess that Mr. Mencken seems to me the closest parallel to some of the most influential writers in colonial New England, I should be laughed at, no doubt justly, though my statement would remain from my viewpoint quite true. When I am misguided enough to find ridiculous the Procrustean attempts of certain critics to put most of the writers of nineteenth century New England to bed in a cramped four-poster labeled the Puritan tradition, there are voices enough to denounce my skepticism. One of the risks of dying has always been that one's sainthood or villainy might not convince pos-

[5] The quotations are from a letter by Joseph Lee printed in the *Boston Herald*, April 15, 1924.

terity, and the Puritans have fared hardly in this respect. Their virtues and vices have been so variously
interpreted as to make any self-conscious ghost uneasy
to a degree. If Puritanism still eludes the scientific analyst, how can its reflection in literature, inevitably less
precise than its religious and political manifestations, be
observed at all?

Perhaps it cannot. Certainly I think it cannot yet be
measured completely. But even a glimpse at the truth
may be welcome. For nearly a century most of the writing done in America was done by Puritans. Puritan boys
grew up and went westward, settled new towns, perhaps
wrote books, and certainly helped to educate the children of new communities. Thus they stamped upon
parts of the ever-moving frontier the impress of a die
cut in New England by the strong hands of Puritans.
The lines might be worn; sometimes the seal was altered
to fit new spaces, but apparently, speaking in the broadest terms, the social and political ideals of the Puritan
colonies—and it may be added, with but mild trepida-
tion, their literary culture—were writ large in America
for generations. If literary history is to be written as it
should be, those who write it must look in literature for
traces of the Puritan turn of mind which in other fields
left so bold a mark.

The Puritan tradition must be that handed down by

the people historically called Puritans. If Victorianism is in question—always assuming there is some one who can define Victorianism—or Presbyterianism, or Methodism, or capitalism, it is better to say so rather than to make the vague doubly vague by stretching a useful historical term to cover what it only loosely fits. Unfortunately even the historians disagree as to the meaning of the name Puritan, and no one of their definitions covers all the groups, all the shades of thought, all the human aspirations which contributed to the making of Puritanism in the broad aspect which alone matters where literature is concerned. Minute differences in polity do not usually affect literature; it is only when an attitude toward life is arresting enough to influence the lives of many men of many formal creeds and divergent standards of worship that it is likely to be mirrored in what they write. The literary student needs a definition generous enough to include John Robinson, Roger Williams, Nathaniel Ward, Bradford, and Winthrop, as well as Baxter, Bunyan, Milton, and Marvell, and comprehensive enough to cover Plymouth Separatists as well as Massachusetts Independents, Congregationalists, Baptists, and Seekers—all the sects which, taken together, make up Puritanism as a school of thought opposed to the way of thinking summed up in the names Anglican and Catholic. No narrower definition can be of much use in explaining the radical separation between the literary creeds and achievements of, say, Crashaw and Anne Bradstreet, Milton and Jeremy Taylor, or Ward and Thomas Morton, the lovable wastrel of Merrymount.

Webster gives a starting point, calling a Puritan "one who, in the time of Queen Elizabeth and the first two Stuarts, opposed traditional and formal usages, and advocated simpler forms of faith and worship than those established by law." This definition is usually extended, and was extended in the seventeenth century, to apply to the whole body of English nonconformists, and even a few nominal conformists, who insisted upon "the personal relation between God and man," hated "professional religion," and tried to base theology and polity on the letter of the Bible, rejecting those elements in the Catholic tradition which seemed to them to be human innovations in the doctrine and practice established by the Apostles.[6] Though he called on Calvin for aid, and usually accepted his theology and at times his political theories, the Puritan asserted the individual's right to read and interpret the Bible for himself, setting this principle against that of the Anglican for whom the church was in a measure both the mediator between God and man and the final interpreter of the Scriptures.

[6] H. O. Wakeman, *The Church and the Puritans*, 5th ed., 1897, p. 56.

"Puritanism was demonstrating the value of a religion . . . based less on tradition than on profound personal convictions of individual religion." [7] Hence came the multiplicity of Puritan sects and the occasional services of Puritanism in the cause of intellectual freedom. It has been said that all men in all times have been divided into conformists and nonconformists, into those who reverence tradition, submerge the individual in the organization, and set form in religion above life, and those for whom man's own relation to God is the center, and individual inquiry, not corporate dogma, is the key to truth.[8] According to this hypothesis, Puritanism was an expression in a given historical period, of the nonconformist spirit.

But Puritanism in New England underwent a swift evolution. In Dr. Rowe's words, it was first "a movement of dissent" but speedily "crystallized into an institution with authority." [9] By 1700 New England Congregationalists were, to be sure, still Puritans in creed and polity, but they had replaced too much of the enthusiasm and intellectual freedom of the founders by reverence for mere system. In other words the essence of the nonconformist spirit was lost; the later New

[7] H. K. Rowe, *History of Religion in the United States*, 1924, p. 31.
[8] H. W. Clark, *History of English Nonconformity*, 1911-13, Vol. I, pp. 1-19.
[9] Rowe, p. 15.

England Puritans may well be called conformists in the broad sense, and not nonconformists at all. This raises new barriers to the discovery of the nature of the Puritan tradition in our literature. Puritanism was not the same thing in the same place at different times; it was not the same in different places at the same time.[10] Is its tradition that of the Independent, with his leanings toward tolerance and democracy, or that of the Presbyterian with his rigid code and confining organization? Is it the tradition of Cotton Mather or of Roger Williams? Of Massachusetts, Rhode Island, or Connecticut? Of 1640 or 1725?

Recognizing the constant need for qualification and for using terms as generally as may be, what can be said of the characteristics of the New England Puritanism which presumably bequeathed something to American literature? In theology the Puritans were usually Calvinists, and the Calvinistic conception of God, the belief in predestination, the absence of free will, and the arbitrary division of mankind into the elect and the damned, the conviction that Heaven and Hell are the ultimate realities, are far-reaching enough to shape many sides

---

[10] "From very early days New England divided into three diverse groups journeying to their Utopias by different roads. Massachusetts Bay, Connecticut, and Rhode Island, were variant answers to the question of what might be expected to result from the domestication in a new environment of the inchoate idealisms of English Puritanism." V. L. Parrington, *Main Currents in American Thought,* 1927, Vol. I, p. 26.

of man's view of life. With the idea of the absolute monarchy of God went an equally energetic visualization of
Satan, captain of evil, and an active meddler in human
affairs. Belief in direct intervention of the Almighty
and the Devil in the daily life of Man explains part of
the Puritan's attitude on how history should be written
and read: "In Reading of all History, ever now and
then make a convenient Pause; to think, *What can I see
of the Glorious* GOD *in these Occurrences?* And always
remember, *The Providence of the Glorious* GOD *in gov-
erning the World, is now under my Contemplation.*" [11]

Just here, however, a qualification becomes necessary.
Much that the Puritans believed, certainly their confidence of the direct power of God and Satan in this
world, was believed as well by non-Puritans. To say that
an interest in "remarkable providences" or in the Devil's
employment of witches is a strictly Puritan characteristic is to make the Puritans sole owners of what was
the common property of most Protestants two or three
centuries ago. Again, we read: "It was to the Scriptures that every Puritan turned to ascertain the will of
God upon every detail of daily life. This obviously
opened the way to the most far-reaching tyranny to
which men could be called upon to submit. . . . The
conformity forced upon individuals by established

[11] C. Mather, *Manuductio ad Ministerium*, 1726, p. 59.

churches had left to the individual his whole freedom
outside of the limited relations to the establishment and
its doctrines. But the Puritan left no such free spaces
in life." [12] But an Anglican historian of the established
church against which the Puritans protested says of that
church at the very time when Massachusetts was being
founded: "The discipline of the Church was brought to
bear upon every department of the life of a generation
that was little fitted to receive it. It interfered with a
man's management of his household, with his trade, with
his amusements, as well as with his religious life and religious duties." [13] Doctors disagree, and there is surely
room for caution in ascribing to Puritanism things which
may have been as much a part of Protestantism in general or of Anglicanism, as of the Congregational or
Presbyterian code.

Indeed, such caution is necessary when one is tempted
to think of Calvinism as an exclusively Puritan theology. Not all Puritans were Calvinists, and certainly
not all Calvinists were Puritans. None the less it may be
said without too many reservations that the essentials
of Calvinistic doctrine so far as they could affect literature are involved in the Puritan tradition. Thence come
a relative contempt for this world, for external nature,

[12] Adams, p. 79.
[13] Wakeman, p. 133. Cf. also Mary Coate, *Social Life in Stuart England*,
1925, pp. 51-2.

for delights of the senses, and a preoccupation with the task of obeying the rigid edicts of an all-powerful God whose will was expressed once and for all in Holy Writ. What did liberty of conscience weigh against the belief that God would have His kingdom grow and that therefore orthodoxy must be secured even if force had to be employed? Intolerance resulted, and indifference to much that a pagan or a non-Calvinist might have welcomed. But perhaps there were gains as well as losses. The Calvinist at least saw beyond the demands and desires of this world and the flesh, and the range of his dreams was the wider and his realization of the mystery and grandeur of one kind of truth, the more keen. Even his introspection had its uses, for Puritan biography, like Puritan autobiography, did not concern itself merely with deeds and battles and worldly success. It must, if it was to express its writers, deal with motives, with inner natures, with the soul, and it is probably no accident that the most interesting and the most "modern" of seventeenth century biographies were written by divines or about divines, and that several of the best are Puritan in attitude. They are not duplicated in America, but even in the colonial Puritans' sketches of their colleagues or ancestors there is the same desire for character as opposed to mere action, for the analysis of personality to which, from quite different motives,

the biographer of the present turns so large a share of
his attention.

That Puritanism was in part a political movement, or,
at least, a type of thought with definite consequences
in politics, needs no argument. And one of these consequences, at least, seems important for the historian of
literature. In the New England colonies the godly, the
professors of religion, the learned, had, at first, the
privileges and rights in both church and state. The
rest of the colonists were more or less definitely subordinated to them. The aristocracy was an aristocracy based
on other than material claims. Intellectual activity and
literary production centered about the meeting-houses
and their congregations. Now a state governed by the
more bookish should prove better suited to the uses of
men of letters than one in which property alone spelled
power, and in which, as has since been the case more
than once, books and scholarship have appealed to the
rulers far less than the interests of the market-place. To
some extent, therefore, the original political system of
Puritan New England fertilized its soil for literature.
Perhaps it is fair to reckon in the Puritan tradition a respect for books and bookmen, for letters and for scholarship, greater than that prevalent outside of New
England during the first years of the colonies. And in
his government the Puritan provided for education on

something like a truly democratic basis. Imaginative creation may be independent of formal schooling, but literary history has always been largely concerned with books distinguished by good craftsmanship, clear thought, and sound learning, qualities the appearance of which is largely determined by the general level of education.

In the mixture of Puritanism were not only theology and theories which bore on politics but also traits of the social class from which came some of its most striking aspirations and conventions. It was a middle class movement. When an Anglican of Charles II's court amiably referred to the Puritans as *"ignorant, stiff-necked, Children of Belial* . . . ever prone to *despise Dominion,* to *speak evil of Dignities,* to *gain-say Order, Rule,* and *Authority;* who have accounted it their honor to contend with *Kings* and *Governors* . . . breathing . . . *sedition* and *calumnies* against the establisht Government . . . hating, despising, or disrespecting the *Nobility, Gentry,* and *Superiour Clergy,"* he was thinking in terms of social class against social class.[14] Richard Baxter, defending his Puritanical tenets, wrote to an Anglican, "Had I never been a Pastor nor lived out of a College . . . I might have thought as you do. And had you converst with as many country people as I have done,

[14] E. Chamberlayne, *Angliae Notitia,* 10th ed., 1677.

and such country-people I think you would have thought as I do." [15] Country people and provincial store-keepers were not the men to make mystics; the beauty of the Catholic tradition and the esthetic side of the worship of the Church of England too often left them cold. The social constitution of the Puritan party made for plain speech for plain men. A famous Massachusetts minister had a "way of Preaching" which was "plain, aiming to shoot his Arrows not over his people's heads, but into their Hearts and Consciences." [16] He knew his audience, and it was the character of the Puritan audience which dictated most Puritan writing.

Then, too, from the Puritans' class came some of their ideals of conduct. Their economic status determined much in their code. They believed in material prosperity, and in working to attain it; they were not tender toward the lazy or incompetent. Discipline, duty, and thrift were beacons, and whether or not they were kindled by the religious side of Puritanism, it was by their light that the Puritan chose to walk. To remember this is doubly valuable, for it calls to mind that much which characterizes early New England and its expansion westward may be in no exact sense the product of

[15] R. Baxter, letter to Henry Dodwell, August 5, 1673, quoted in F. J. Powicke, *The Reverend Richard Baxter—Under the Cross* (1662-1691), 1927, p. 224.
[16] I. Mather, *Life . . . of . . . Richard Mather*, 1850, p. 85.

Puritanism but simply the resultant of economic and social forces in themselves quite independent of the historical Puritans. Middle class standards were not peculiar to New England nor was its economic organization. If so, some things which we lay at the door of Puritanism might have existed had there been no Puritans in America, provided the social and economic conditions of early New England—and perhaps its eccentric climate—had been elsewhere and at other times reproduced. Writing of New England, Edwin Arlington Robinson says:

> Wonder begets an envy of all those
> Who boil elsewhere with such a lyric yeast
> Of love that you will hear them at a feast
> Where demons would appeal for some repose,
> Still clamoring where the chalice overflows
> And crying wildest who have drunk the least.
> Passion is here a soilure of the wits.[17]

Longfellow's avoidance of outspoken emotion in his poems is well known; he wrote once, "The real trials of our lives are for the most part unseen by others. Our temptations . . . are in the desert. The world around us knows little of them, and cares less." [18] Emerson's

[17] E. A. Robinson, "New England," in *Dionysus in Doubt*, 1925, p. 90. Quoted by permission of The Macmillan Company.
[18] Letter to John Neal, August 4, 1854, a copy of which was given me by Professor I. T. Richards of the University of Maine.

*Journals* show his terseness in moments of grief. And in what the Puritan wrote for publication there is constant reticence about his more intimate experience. No one need take seriously pronouncements that a lack of emotion characterizes the Puritans and the inheritors from them, but there is good reason to wonder whether chariness about displaying one's feelings before others is not the mark of their breed.[19]   Yet Puritanism may not be at the root of it; Quakers share the trait, and there are other men the deep waters of whose natures show no ripple on the surface. Was the Anglican, Richard Hooker, a Puritan when he wrote of God that "our safest eloquence concerning him, is our silence. . . . He is above, and we upon earth; therefore it behoveth our words to be wary and few." [20] Is instinctive reserve in the face of what is most deeply moving born of Calvinism or Puritanism, or is it simply the mark of racial temperament or the standard of a social class? May it not have been fostered by a frontier life in which discipline and self-reliance were the best armory and man was constantly aware of how closely a deaf

[19] Cf. Emerson's, "In all things I would have the island of man inviolate. . . . No degree of affection need invade this religion. . . . Coolness and absence of heat indicate fine qualities. A gentleman makes no noise; a lady is serene." *Essays, Second Series*, Concord ed., p. 137. Quoted by permission of Houghton Mifflin Company.
[20] Richard Hooker, *Works*, Oxford, 1807, Vol. I, p. 200.

Fate in the shape of storm, disease, and famine, dogged his heels?

For the founders of New England literature what mattered most were religious truths and moral values. All else took second place before their delight in the vision which was to them holiness and the way of God. They were not saints—Heaven forfend—nor were all of them sincere or virtuous, but their leaders were engrossed with their own spiritual welfare and with their thrilling pursuit of what they construed as the Christian ideal in faith and conduct. There is more than one kind of beauty, and the Puritan, like many other men in all ages, discovered in what he saw as the beauty of holiness enough to satisfy all the cravings of his nature. His life seems sterile to us. Perhaps it was so in fact; perhaps we fail to appreciate how passionate was his conviction and how challenging his ideal. While Puritanism was alive, with power to make history, its morality and its rules were developed from within as the fruit of individual faith. Later the rules persisted, but the whole meaning of morality was changed. Then laws were imposed from without and observed because they always had been. The individual must conform to the mold, without his ancestors' privilege of living under laws and among institutions which were not lifeless monuments but the flowers of an earnestly cherished

conviction and of an ardent adoration of beauty, holiness, and truth. Thus Emerson seems the Puritan. He
revolted against dead form and system; his test for
everything was rooted in the moral, and he preached
always the morality which proceeds from the sincere
belief of the individual transcending law merely as law.
He is nearer, I think, to the original Puritan tradition
than the writers of his day and later who seem to have
followed a ready made code external to themselves and
by no means the product of their own aspiring toward
truth. The difference between Puritanism and what
passes for Victorianism might be measured by the contrast between Emerson and Longfellow. Perhaps there
are two divisions of the Puritan tradition in respect to
all this: one, the heritage of later Puritanism, which
welds rules into systems, and the other, nearer to the
nonconformist spirit of the first settlers on Massachusetts shores, which also makes moral values and Biblical
precept supreme, but conceives of them not merely as
grim idols cut in the stone of inherited reverence but
as part of the expression of the enthusiasm and rich-
ness of the spirit of man. This view dethroned kings
and settled wildernesses, and must be implicit in a Puritan tradition worthy of the name.

Sometime or other there must be faced the old chimera
of the Calvinist and Puritan who hated art in all its

forms. The Puritans closed the theaters and desecrated English cathedrals, *ergo* they were contemners of all artistic creation. The formula is too simple to be true. Congress in 1774, when it was by no means a Puritan body, did what amounted to closing the theaters in this country, but was moved simply by a desire to encourage "frugality" by discouraging "every species of extravagance and dissipation." [21] Retainers of Henry VIII ravaged cathedrals, but thus far no one has declared Anglicanism and its tradition to be bound up with hostility toward art. Puritan authors, even in the colonies, often adopted literary fashions current among the *littérateurs* of England, though they must have known that to do so was to take a leaf out of the artist's book. They struggled with verse and aspired to poetry, even though they realized that poetry was an art. Cotton Mather, prescribing for candidates for the ministry, discusses music without hostility, and recommends both the reading and writing of poetry. He took pains to write his theory of prose style, and like other Puritan historians, tried to lay down rules for the writing of history, by no means leaving out of account its literary aspect. What is lacking among the Puritans is any whole-hearted or exclusive devotion to art in any form. For them other

[21] A. H. Quinn, *History of the American Drama from the Beginning to the Civil War*, 1923, p. 32.

things in life came first. The Muses are jealous mis-
tresses, and the Puritan artist was too seldom inspired
by the fire of their greatest votaries, but he did not
spurn them and now and then gave them a sincere if
timid greeting.

Nor can it be safely said that whatever lack of literary
merit there may be in the writings of early New England is wholly the fault of Puritanism applied to art. The
contrast between the blind Milton, writing *Paradise Lost*
in retirement, and Milton, the Latin Secretary, turning
out controversial prose, points the moral. The Puritan in
the fray, fighting for his principles, knew that one
pamphlet, bristling with argument, served better than
a dozen epics, however grandly conceived. And Puritans were rarely beyond the need for controversy. Baxter's comment on his own books sums up the case: "I
scarce ever wrote one Sheet twice over, nor stayed to
make any Blots or Interlinings, but was fain to let it
go as it was first conceived. . . . Some sudden Oc-
casions or other extorted almost all my Writings from
me." [22] Moreover, the colonial Puritan was not only a
Puritan embroiled in controversy with adroit opponents,
but a colonist and, at first, a frontiersman. The Puritan
colonies in America were not alone in leaving small
mark on literature; their neighbors did no better. It may

[22] M. Sylvester, *Reliquiae Baxterianae,* 1696, Part I, p. 124.

be that Puritanism is not solely to blame; possibly only supermen could—or can—nurture art in the wilderness.

The Puritans did write much, and the kernel of all their work is the same. Their preoccupation with religion and morality dictated the subject matter and mood; they left humor and the external beauty of this world out of account as too trivial to waste precious paper and ink upon. The tone of authority in most of their pages is redolent of their political system, which made the learned the leaders of the flock. They did not speculate freely about some things which we call into question, and their imagination is not of the sort which makes romantic poets or great painters of Utopias. But even staunch Calvinists loved to discuss theological problems, unsolved and perhaps insoluble, and in so doing they gave their intellects relatively free play. It took real imaginative power to write of God, of Satan, of Heaven, and of Hell in the true Puritan vein. The right to read and interpret the Bible for oneself, an essential tenet of original Puritanism, involved the right to reject authorities which were often in other circles still revered.[23] Even when the authority of the Bible

[23] Mr. Henson makes an interesting comment in his *Studies in English Religion in the Seventeenth Century* (1903, pp. 51-2): "The Puritan deferred to an authority, which . . . was, in the last analysis, the authority of his own reason and conscience. . . . He could unlearn his own errors and undo his own mistakes, for the authority which determined his course was that of his own understanding, and that grew wiser and more trustworthy under the disciplines of life."

itself, or of Calvin, intervened, the possibility of interpreting any sentence in two ways stood the Puritan in
good stead and saved him from a too confining allegiance to the letter of any text! However uninviting
most of his pages may be, he did at times, especially in
biography and history, make his words endure.

The Puritans' idealism lies back of much of their
work. But since they were men of affairs, their idealism
is closely tied in with daily life, and nothing in their
writing is more amusing and more significant than their
curious juxtapositions of religion and common sense, the
visions of faith and the consciousness of everyday fact.
Samuel Sewall at a picnic sees a glass of liquor upset
and instantly moralizes on the fragility and mortality
of man; Cotton Mather occupies himself in linking
pious meditations with the commonest daily acts. The
effect is often absurd, but it comes, after all, from the
same impulse which gave Bunyan his strength—from
the belief that there was no barrier between religion and
life. Bunyan wrote of a spiritual pilgrimage in terms of
a journey through seventeenth century England; the
landscape of Bedfordshire and the idiom of plain men
served him for the revelation of religious truth. "Practical idealism" has been called an element of Americanism; if the phrase applies anywhere it applies to much
that is ridiculous and sublime in Puritan literature. To
satisfy a pious colonist a book must work; it must teach,

console, or record what should not be forgotten.[24] This is the practical side; the idealism comes out in confidence that truth is the Grail, that the eternal mysteries are the ultimate realities. Truth versus fiction, work versus play, faith versus fact—such phrases go far to explain Puritan literature.

The style in which the Puritan wrote shows something of him. The influence of the Bible is everywhere, and there are repeated pleas for simplicity, for plain writing and direct phrasing. Part of this came from the social character of the Puritan audience, and part from what seems to be a distrust of useless ornamentation and of style for style's sake. Richard Mather eschewed "obscure phrases" and "Exotick Words" because he looked "upon the affectation of such things" as savoring of "Carnal wisdom." [25] Baxter said: "The *Truths of God* do perform their work more by *their Divine Authority*, and *proper Evidence* and *material Excellency*, than by any *ornaments* of *fleshly wisdom*; and (as *Seneca* saith) though I will not despise an *elegant Physicion*, yet will I not think my self much the happyer for his adding eloquence to his healing art." [26] John Cotton, preaching as

[24] Cf. Richard Baxter's remark on some of his own verses: "(Being now too dull for poetry) they take not with those that expect more art—they profit two sorts, women and vulgar Christians and persons in passion and affliction." Quoted in Powicke, p. 276.

[25] I. Mather, p. 85.

[26] R. Baxter, *A Saint or a Brute*, 1662, introductory epistle, p. 3.

an Anglican in England, "used such Florid Strains, as
extremely recommended him unto *the most,* who rel-
ished the *Wisdom of Words* above the *Words of Wisdom";* but when he became a Puritan he felt it his
"Duty to preach with such a *Plainness,* as became the
*Oracles* of God, which are intended for the Conduct of
Men in the *Paths of Life,* and not for *Theatrical* Osten-
tations and Entertainments." [27]

The attitude behind these quotations should not be
confused with a liking for bad prose. Bunyan alone
should prevent that. His brethren in America had now
and then a sense of the power of simplicity, which is
after all the basis of much great art. I think that no
later historian has ever told the story of the Pilgrims
with as much emotional effect as William Bradford.
Perhaps he was merely lucky; but the good luck which
clothes a great experience in memorable words is after
all one of the things we mean by art. It is the very
discipline and stark simplicity of Bradford's best pages
which make them thrilling. To say there was no art in
his pages is to confuse art and artificiality. Of course
there were many inexperienced craftsmen among colonial authors. They were misled by bad models and occasionally failed the more miserably because their am-
bition was greater than their skill. Poor Edward John-

[27] C. Mather, *Magnalia,* 1702, Book III, Chapter I, Paragraphs 4, 6.

son built his history on a great conception, and in Bunyan's hands his allegory might have burned with divine fire. But he undertook more than he could accomplish, and his *Wonder Working Providence,* just because it is by no means a success and yet not wholly a failure, reveals both the vision and the blindness of the Puritan turned artist.

In all this there may be a few points which help to identify the Puritan tradition as a strain in our literary history, but it cannot be too often repeated that any attempt at present to define this tradition rigidly or to treat it as a completely separable entity, is futile. It is more valorous than discreet to turn to nineteenth century books and declare: "This is Puritan; that is not. This has a strong tincture of Puritanism; that, no trace." To ask a few questions is to see the danger. Was Unitarianism the child of the nonconforming spirit of the Puritans or a traitor in their camp? Is repressive legislation today the heritage of the old New England ideal or a negation of that ideal in its emphasis upon morality imposed from without? Is Hawthorne a Puritan because he is fascinated by moral problems, or does his subjecting of these problems to artistic tests suffice to divorce him from his ancestral tradition? An American poet wrote of nature:

> For the pains, the fever, and the fret
> Engendered of a weak, unquiet heart,
> She hath no solace; and who seeks her when
> These be the troubles over which he moans,
> Reads in her unreplying lineaments
> Rebukes that, to the guilty consciousness,
> Strike like contempt.[28]

Was he a Puritan, though he lived in South Carolina? Was the flourishing of historiography in nineteenth century New England born of the Puritans' zeal in the same art? Was the revolutionary ardor of Massachusetts in 1775 the outgrowth of imported romanticism, of economic and social conditions, or, as more than one of the patriots suggested, of inherited Puritan ideals? Were the nineteenth century didactic poets and novelists direct heirs of Puritanism, or was their attitude toward morality different from that which the colonists derived from their ardent faith? Many such questions might be answered; many more have been, usually in more or less contradictory ways, but most tax too hardly our present knowledge. Puritan and Puritanism are tyrannous words which rule the more absolutely because they connote so little that can be defined.

But present doubts should make for future certain-

[28] Henry Timrod, "The Summer Bower," in *Poems*, 1899, p. 108.

ties. If scholars, critics, and writers will turn to Puritanism and its bequests with a recognition of the nature and complexity of the subject, new vistas may be opened. As Professor Foerster has pointed out, to know the Puritan we must know the Cavaliers, and we must know something of the traditions of his race and class, as well as of the customs and standards of his century and of the land in which he lived. Above all we need immensely more knowledge of what the Puritans wrote. There are enough general treatments of colonial literature and summary criticisms of Puritan writing, but I know of none, except Mr. Tyler's, which is based on anything like a complete acquaintance with the material. Before the Puritan tradition can be intelligently written of, before the history of colonial literature or of American literature in general can be written as they deserve to be, Puritan books must be read, and with them at least a selection of those put forth by their contemporaries at home and abroad. There must be more acquaintance with what they read. Historians must tell more of the details of daily life in the colonies, the details which everywhere affect subtly but powerfully what men set down in books. There is great need for biographies of colonists—not biographies of the surface-skimming type, essaying character analysis without much interest in the evidence—but biographies telling all that can be discovered of what their subjects did, believed, and dreamed, and covering the thousand unconsidered trifles which always enter into a finished and truthful portrait. Studies of books, of groups of books, and of types of writing, as well as accurate reprints of colonial texts, are indispensable. When such work has been done, for Puritans and Cavaliers, North and South, for America of 1640 and 1750 as well as 1860, the critic may for the first time feel sure of his ground. And the artist must play his part. Early America and its men and women appear in novels, plays, and essays, but in how few do they come to life! When the artist is at last given raw material for his purpose, he should be able to transmute bare fact into the richer truth born only of the creative imagination.

The Quest is not an easy one. As Longfellow put it: "The stern old puritanical character rises above the common level of life; it has a breezy air about its summits, but they are bleak and forbidding." [29] But Professor Parrington gives a word of consolation: "The colonial period is meager and lean only to those whose 'disedged appetites' find no savor in old-fashioned beef and puddings. . . . No other path leads so directly into the heart of those old days as the thorny path of their theological and political controversies; and if one

[29] S. Longfellow, *Life of Henry W. Longfellow*, 1891, Vol. III, p. 412.

will resolutely pick his way amongst the thorns, he will have his reward in coming close to the men who debated earnestly over the plans and specifications of the Utopia that was to be erected in the free spaces of America, and who however wanting they may have been in the lesser arts, were no mean architects and craftsmen for the business at hand." [30] There are compensations, certainly, for any one who will read colonial literature with a catholic appreciation of all it has to offer, nor are esthetic values always to seek. If the *Magnalia,* Bradford's *History,* Winthrop's letters, Ward's *Simple Cobler,* and Anne Bradstreet's *Contemplations,* were taken away, the loss to great literature, in the strictest sense, would be small; but the reader who has learned to find more than one source of enjoyment in books, appreciates the good as well as the great, and can discover the best even when it is half buried by the less worthy, would have real cause to mourn.

What the goal of the study of the Puritan tradition will be, it is too early to say. Perhaps the weaknesses, pettinesses, and unlovelinesses of Puritanism were dominant in it, and its tradition may prove to have been of evil tenor. But the search itself must be worth while. It must lead through little explored realms, full of strange sights for modern eyes. Nor is there much doubt that

[30] Parrington, Vol. I, p. vii.

when it does become possible to speak with reasonable confidence of the Puritan literary tradition and its implications, some of the old landmarks will be seen in new lights. The patriotic writers of the Revolution, Emerson, Melville, Hawthorne, and Longfellow, Whitman and Emily Dickinson, Thoreau and Wendell Phillips, Robert Frost and Vachel Lindsay, Sinclair Lewis and H. L. Mencken—even familiar names may take on new meanings. Given fresh insight into continuing traditions and inherited forces and fresh realization of what American Puritanism with all its linked sympathies and antagonisms has meant for literature, we may evoke from the best thumbed of our books flashes of significance hitherto unseen. Good or bad, the American past is ours. Whether we read or write, it jogs our elbows. By seeing better other men who read and wrote in an earlier America we may see further into the life which hedges us about. In scanning their horizons we may find breadth added to our own.

# VI. THE ROMANTIC MOVEMENT

## PAUL KAUFMAN

A GENERATION ago, in the last decade of the nineteenth century, the laconic announcement of the
passing of the frontier inspired an interpretation of
American civilization almost as novel and sweeping as
the pioneer movement itself. Today we accept the facts
which this interpretation has illumined and arranged in
panoramic perspective; we recognize thé unique shaping
influence of the frontier, in its various aspects and meaning, upon our national outlook and upon our literature.

In the same decade American scholarship produced
the first volumes recognizing and describing in English
literature a movement which was then beginning to be
termed romantic. And since that time the designation
has persisted, however controversially, as the counter of
criticism and literary history. Yet only within a year or
two has any one definitely proposed that in American
letters also could be discovered a "romantic" period.[1]

[1] First by the editor of this volume, as indicated by the divisions "The
Advance of Romanticism" and "The Height of the Romantic Movement"
in *American Poetry and Prose*, 1925; and by Professor Parrington's comprehensive interpretation, *The Romantic Revolution in America, 1800-1860*
(Vol. II of *Main Currents in American Thought*), 1927.

Hitherto we have called our literature between the Revolutionary and the Civil Wars by the noncommittal chronological name Early National, or we have made geographical divisions and naturally spoken of the New England school or the New York group; and if we have hazarded a descriptive epithet at all we have spoken of our "classic period." Inner coherence, prevailing tendencies we have not discovered or at least been willing to conceive in terms universally applied to contemporary European literature in the earlier part of the nineteenth century.

That our prose fiction and drama during this period was romantic is well recognized. That the most conspicuous single concerted movement, Transcendentalism, was romantic in a different sense, that it represents the most complete counterpart of various European romanticisms, is equally clear. That the personalities of the time which appear now as the most important, Emerson, Thoreau, Hawthorne, Poe, Melville, Whitman, likewise embodied in their several fashions new movements which we label romantic cannot be questioned. Still we have hesitated to apply the inclusive designation, partly perhaps because our literature has seemed at once so diverse and so largely imitative, formal, reticent. At all events we have not seen an underlying unity which would warrant the single descriptive term applied to European literatures.

Not even although America has traditionally incarnated the romantic in almost every sense. Not even although we still speak with reason of the American adventure, the great democratic experiment, both of which are the essence of romanticism. But is it not strange that the migratory impulse which sprang from revolt against the disintegrating authorities and institutions of Europe and which found unique opportunity for unlimited expression should not have been called romantic? For American civilization detaching itself from the old world and developing new forms of social life has been essentially a quest, the most recent racial struggle for individual freedom. Its distinctive type is represented by the pioneer with boundless opportunity stretching out before him in every direction and ever-expanding frontiers luring him on. What could be more romantic? Nothing, assuredly, at least to men of the old world from the moment when the marvels of the tropical wilderness first broke upon their view; and still at the present time, when we are reproached for our vulgarity and greed, we are to them as romantic in the Volstead Act and in our reckless waste as once we were in our scenery and our capture of a continent.

But perhaps we may urge that the spirit of freedom

and experiment has so thoroughly pervaded American civilization that no single period can properly be termed romantic. This is only partially true. Since the war between the states we have become an increasingly bourgeois industrial empire immersed in the business of getting on. Prior to the war of independence the settlers along the seaboard were still transplanted Europeans looking backward rather than forward and not inspired with visions of great adventure or with passion for experiment. Can we then find in the intervening early national epoch a prevailing spirit which distinguishes it from the other two? Recent historical criticism has formulated just such a distinction and two volumes bear witness in their titles to belief in the new historical orientation: one boldly proclaims its belief in "the romantic revolution" [2] and the other announces that "the golden day" dawned, flourished, and waned. It was, says Mr. Mumford, "the period of an Elizabethan daring on the sea, of a well-balanced adjustment of farm and factory in the East, of a thriving regional culture . . . an age in which the American mind had flourished and had begun to find itself. . . . The Civil War cut a white gash through the history of the country. . . . When the curtain rose on the post-bellum scene this old

[2] The work cited above.

America was for all practical purposes demolished." [3]

So, too, most recent historians have found unity in an age of diverse and tumultuous expansion. The Jacksonian consummation of the ideal of complete political equality arrived significantly in the very middle of the period, and the last barriers of aristocratic control in both traditional and newer senses were swept away. This all-important revolution, combined with sudden floods of immigration, the spread of industrialism, and the westward migrations, produced "vigorous mass movements marked by lectures, public schools, circuses, museums, penny newspapers, varied propaganda, political caucuses, woman suffrage conventions, temperance reform, labor organization, Mormonism, Millerism, mesmerism—the martial notes of the agitator mingled with the vibrant tones of the moralist, preacher, and educator—pioneers in opinion marching forward, sometimes inspired, often ignorant and usually crotchety, to the conquest of the future in America." [4] As Professor Parrington has written: "It needs no uncommon eyes, surely, to discover in the swift changes that came to America in the wake of the second English war, the seed-bed of those ebullient romanticisms which in politics and economics, in theology and literature, turned

---

[3] Lewis Mumford, *The Golden Day*, 1926, pp. 158-9.

[4] Charles and Mary Beard, *The Rise of American Civilization*, 2 vols., 1927, Vol. I, p. 728.

away so contemptuously from the homespun past. . . .
The ideal of a static society having been put away, progress was assumed to be the first law of nature, and in-
novation was accepted as the sign and seal of progress.
It was our first great period of exploitation, and from it
emerged . . . the spirit of romance, gross and tawdry
in vulgar minds, dainty and refined in the more cultivated. . . . But always romance." [5]

Granted, then, that this period manifests a persistent
impulse of enthusiastic expansion in every field of American activity, do we find a corresponding expression of
coherent character in literature? An answer in the
affirmative depends upon the recognition of the fact
that American romanticism is both imitative and independent, exhibiting all degrees between extremes—to
take major personalities, between Longfellow and Whitman in poetry or between Irving and Emerson in prose.
The differences between these two in both instances are
comprehensive: in content, in form, and in temper.
But the mere mention of these names raises the fundamental question of defining the limits of romanticism.[6]
Rather obviously, an initial confusion has arisen from
the elementary ambiguity of the adjective which must

[5] *Op. cit.*, p. v.
[6] The problem of definition has been analyzed by the present writer in
"Defining Romanticism: A Survey and a Program," MLN, XL, No. 4
(April, 1925). In the present survey I have for obvious reasons avoided
the controversial and used a classification generally recognized.

refer both to romance and romanticism. By the first
we mean either the temper or the expression in literature of some form of idealization, of departure from
the commonplace and portrayal of the exceptional, the
marvelous, the mysterious; of life conceived in high
colors and in more striking aspects. This we mean when
we characterize the American drama and prose fiction
during the period in question as romantic. But the romantic movement in Europe expresses far more than
this quality; and no simple formula will comprehend its
varied impulses. Let us say that it includes a recovery
of the past as an effort to broaden emotional and imaginative outlooks; the revolt against tradition and
authority in whatever area of human concern; humanitarian sympathy including new interests in humble life
and assertion of individual rights; a fresh perception of
nature; the renascence of wonder; and in general an
ascendancy of feeling and imagination.[7] And all these
we may properly apply in testing American literature.
To these we may add what we may call a patriotic romanticism,[8] expressing itself in declarations of literary

[7] Primitivism is omitted because of its conspicuous absence in American
literature.

[8] A significant illustration is found in the assertion of Joseph Perkins'
commencement "Oration upon Genius" at Harvard in 1797: "Under the
conditions of such singular felicity, which separate the United States
from the rest of the world, surely genius must be an exotic too delicate
for our climate . . . or it cannot but flourish in a soil like ours." For
the first time in history, he declared, "in a country 'where all men are

independence, which began during the Revolution, and also deliberately expressing American scenes and themes, in which latter respect it bears striking parallel to the first stages of German romanticism.

To analyze these aspects in both major and minor writers, to essay and synthesize, pointing out their absence or prevalence together with indications of originality, is to write the history of the romantic movement of America; and this long-delayed undertaking urgently invites the best efforts of present-day students. Within the present limits I can only outline the approach here suggested and describe the main results. Fortunately the facts are so well recognized that most critical assertions need no demonstration, and hence my assignment is to show the facts in a new setting.

To attempt discovery of the beginnings of American romanticism is even more futile than the same endeavor in English literature. Yet as definite new tendencies appear in England during the third quarter of the eighteenth century, so similar expressions with definite applications to the American scene emerge at the same time. Crèvecœur represents a significant realization of radical differences between the civilizations of the Old and the

born free and equal'—emancipated from the chains of despotism, the eagle of genius is at full liberty to expand her vigorous wings . . . to build her nests among the stars." I called attention to the interest of this utterance in "Heralds of Original Genius," *Essays in Memory of Barrett Wendell*, 1926, pp. 191-222.

New World. In his very question, What is an American? appears new consciousness of the separation which dates from 1620; and his answer that the American is a "new man who acts upon new principles" shows distinctly formulated belief. Crèvecœur is a pioneer in his vision of a material and cultural civilization, rich in promise for all. It is this promise which, with varied emphasis, during the Revolutionary period and the years following, is insistently voiced. In the decorous neoclassical style of Trumbull, Dwight, and Barlow is celebrated the glowing prospect of future glory. In many a Revolutionary song and ballad is more positively proclaimed revolt against tyranny and a new liberty hailed with vigorous enthusiasm. Tom Paine may be claimed for American literature as powerful spokesman of the "common sense" yet none the less novel contention for human rights. And indeed the Declaration of Independence belongs to the same movement.

Among these must be ranked high in importance Philip Freneau, who is the most versatile and pronounced exponent of dawning nationalism, as well as a pioneer in poetic appreciation of the sea, of native Indian civilization, and of natural scenes on the new continent. Beginning as he did in his commencement poem at Princeton on "The Rising Glory of America" before the Revolution and living on to 1832, he represents the most complete embodiment of this period of nationalistic romanticism. In literary importance he is the greatest forerunner of that vigorous independence which is given a universal philosophic sanction by Emerson's "American Scholar" and which culminates in the rhapsodies of Whitman.

The second stage is more distinctly literary and traditional. After the Revolution the three founders of American prose fiction turned to romance in the older sense. Charles Brockden Brown found his models in the Gothic tale which was enjoying wide popularity in Europe and produced American versions designed to inspire entertaining terror. In much more original fashion Cooper was moved to surpass the English stories of stirring adventure, first naturalizing the sea in American prose and then portraying indigenous types of Indian and scout in the light of virile yet romantic idealization. Often vividly faithful in representing details of action and natural environment, he may be most fairly estimated by recalling that to the European readers of his time he seemed to reflect the distinctive romantic elements of the new world scene. Of quite different temperament was Irving who found himself much more at home socially and intellectually in the old world. Deriving his literary nourishment from the urbanity of an Addison, lacking strong convictions, and possessing notably charm of style, he was hardly a romanticist, rather a genial romancer. Yet he does belong to literary romance in his discovery of the old world picturesqueness, notably of course in Spain; and he inaugurated the American tradition of recovering both the European and the American past and presenting them as more or less colorful and glamorous.

Out of these beginnings were developed various types of prose romance which have flourished luxuriantly to the present time. To the early popularity of such fiction significant testimony was recorded by Royall Tyler in his preface to *The Algerine Captive* in 1797 when he observed that after an absence of seven years he was impressed with "the extreme avidity with which books of mere amusement were purchased and perused by all ranks of his countrymen." When he left New England, "books of biography, travels, novels and modern romance were confined to our seaports." But on his return he found "the whole land" filled "with modern travels and novels almost as incredible." In the last decade of the eighteenth century apparently the young nation had discovered romance, which was inevitably imported wholesale from Europe. Tyler deplored the fact that "they are not of our own manufacture," and as if to remove the reproach and meet a new demand, the important writers of the first three decades of the nineteenth century provided the various types of romantic narrative, both imitative and original.

Within two more decades two greater personalities made permanent contributions not only to American but to world literature. Both Hawthorne and Melville were romancers par excellence, both voyaging into strange seas of thought alone, the one exploring intensively the inner realms of the soul, the other ranging extensively over the earth and in his most important work finding a certain cosmic meaning in man's deeds of daring adventure. Hawthorne explicitly termed several of his narratives romance, but into traditional form he infused profound brooding and achieved the new distinction of making romance profoundly subjective. Hitherto this genre both in prose and verse had been, in the psychological phrase of our day, of extrovert nature. He created an original introvert form true to his own character, thus introducing the recent romantic preoccupation with individual feeling and imagination into the traditional type.

Sharing the same aloofness from the American environment and the same passionate artistic impulses, Poe also, with obvious differences, inaugurated his own adaptations of romantic tale, working in his own original technique to produce a *frisson* of the imagination and the feelings both in prose and verse. In his poetry

Poe transcends the spirit of older romance as he catches the new English accent of mystery, vague longing for some shadowy ideal of beauty, and the haunting sense of frustration, found in Coleridge, Shelley, or Keats. Although some of his lyric work is timeless and cannot happily be confined within a formula, his distinctive and perhaps best self is Israfel.

> If I could dwell
> Where Israfel
> Hath dwelt, and he where I,
> He might not sing so wildly well
> A mortal melody,
> While a bolder note than this might swell
> From my lyre within the sky.

In complete contrast stands Longfellow, our most wide-ranging purveyor of European song and story. From Portugal, Spain, and Italy, Germany, Belgium, and France, from Lapland and Scandinavia, he brought rich store and naturalized it all by the hospitable hearth of the New England Wayside Inn. Between him and Poe the difference may be most simply dramatized in the contrast between the two poems of quest and of aspiration, "Eldorado" and "Excelsior": the one earnestly moral, with obvious human theme moving with some metrical ineptitude and commonplace rime to a defi-

nite conventional ending in a Christian setting; the
other quite unmoral, seeking subtle emotional effects by
sheer rhythm and melody, the vague quest unfinished
somewhere in a land of supernatural fantasy. Nor would
I discredit Longfellow. His services to American poetry
are undeniably impressive, and he did far more than
translate European literature. Gracefully and enter-
tainingly he rendered the Indian into romance. He do-
mesticated in mildly and harmlessly sentimental forms
scenes of early colonial days. But except for the handful
of poems on slavery he reveals almost as little interest in
the turbulent expanding civilization about him as did
Poe himself. Although he could appreciate the poetry of
the new European romanticism, he appears to have felt
none of the new powerful impulses which inspired its
spokesmen. He was too much absorbed in the past, both
of Europe and of America. Even nature moved him little. He understood Dante better.

Longfellow represents in graciously academic tone the
milder romance themes which dominate our literature
throughout the whole period. In much cruder fashion
our prose fiction and drama produced a vigorous rank
growth which partially replaced the stream of imported
novels recorded by Royall Tyler. In the preface to *The
Yemassee* (1835) William Gilmore Simms notes that
"modern Romance is the substitute which the people of

the present day offer for the ancient epic," but as Mr. Carl Van Doren has suggested, Simms meant by epic not Homer but Froissart.[9] "The sudden onslaught—the retreat as sudden—the midnight tramp—the moonlight bivouack—the swift surprise—and, amid the fierce and bitter warfare, always, like a sweet star shining above the gloom, the faithful love, the constant prayer, the devoted homage and fond allegiance of the maiden heart"—such was Simms' own cherished formula, which he repeatedly applied to his Revolutionary romances. So, increasingly amid the westward march, romance sprang up in the footsteps of the pioneer. Over the mountains not of the moon but of the Alleghanies lay Eldorados called Kentucky, Ohio, and Wisconsin; and the gallant knights who rode forth were named Daniel Boone and David Crockett. While Hawthorne brooded over the secret ways of the heart in Salem and while Melville roved the South Seas or sought Moby Dick, an increasing number of forgotten chroniclers were discovering new romance in the rude democracy pushing its way toward the Pacific. They were not Dumas or Scotts, but they bore testimony to America's own original romantic movement, which continues in various frontiers to this day.

So too in the drama the tradition of romance, particu-

[9] *Cambridge History of American Literature*, Vol. I, p. 316.

larly in tragedy, was maintained. During the first quarter of the nineteenth century many European themes, ancient and modern, were presented in native versions, but more and more American playwrights turned to the scenes of their own history, producing nearly two hundred plays on American subjects before 1860. "As was natural," observes Professor Quinn, "the Revolution was the most appealing theme. Practically every great event from the Boston Tea Party to the Battle of Yorktown was dramatized." [10] That the stage vogues corresponded to the trend of the prose fiction may be demonstrated by the constant dramatization of the current novels, notably those of Cooper. However conventional and imitative was our theater, American playwrights achieved all that could be expected in presenting native subjects. What concerns us here is the comparatively slight proportion of realistic comedy. The drama was prevailingly romantic.

Amid all this American adaptation of romance in the older meaning, our literature betrays little consciousness of the new powerful forces in Europe until the fourth decade of the century. But when in 1836 the little volume entitled simply *Nature* appeared, we can now see that a certain individualistic impulse of Puritanism, developing for two centuries on American soil

[10] *Ibid.*, Vol. I, p. 225.

and at last expanded by new English and German outlooks, suddenly issued its own original manifesto: "Why
should not we also enjoy an original relation to the universe? . . . There are new lands, new men, new
thoughts. Let us demand our own works and laws and
worship." This earliest vision of Emerson in which his
whole future writing is implicit is at once social, individual, national. In the familiar, more explicitly national
note of the following year, he declared, "Our long apprenticeship to the learning of other lands draws to a
close. The millions that around us are rushing into life
cannot always be fed on the sere remains of foreign
harvests." Likewise, in the same address he exalted
"everything which tends to insulate the individual . . .
so that each man shall feel the world as his, and man
shall treat with man as a sovereign state with a sovereign
state." Each man, he declared, finds the world of truth
in "his own bosom alone." These words, ringing with
new authority, proclaimed that a new romanticism had
arrived in America.

To prove this were unnecessary here, Emerson focuses
in himself most of the important elements of English
romanticism: revolt against tradition and authority and
the assertion of individual rights, the fresh perception
of nature, the renascence of wonder, and the reliance
upon feeling and imagination. Philosophically of course

he assimilated the German doctrine that the world is in-
tuitively created by the individual self, which, together
with the belief that the Over-Soul dwells in every man,
constitutes the core of Transcendentalism. The only elements in the English romanticism lacking in Emerson
were positive humanitarian sympathy and concern with
humble life. Otherwise it is hardly too much to say
that in the range of his writing both in prose and verse
he is a whole romantic movement in himself! He combined both the varied aspects of the English and German movements in an original synthesis which is both a
culmination and, in America, at least, a new inspiration of various movements.

Were it not for this overshadowing importance of
Emerson, half a dozen or more of his contemporary
Transcendentalists would doubtless loom up in more
impressive proportions today. As is well known, several
of them manifested eccentricities characteristic of the
more extreme European romanticists. One went insane,
one followed certain German romanticists into the Roman church, and the leading woman of the group married an Italian count! To stray further from New England norms, intellectual, religious, social, were impossible. Only in their rectitude and moral idealism could
they be called "correct." They were certainly original
and not conventional. And if they left little enduring

literature, some of the more ardent among them dared to attempt the realization of the Coleridgean dream of an earthly Utopia. Perhaps this transitory experiment at Brook Farm is more significant than we think. May it not symbolize the whole democratic experiment in social idealism, romantic in the deepest sense, fulfilling the dream of many centuries?

Just as insurgent as the Transcendentalists but facing everyday actualities with far more vigor and courage, Thoreau takes his place beside Emerson as a prophet of individualism. But his distinction consists in his total lack of mistiness and sentimentalism. As no other American, perhaps no man recorded in history, he committed himself to the belief that "the most live is the wildest" —not in mere craving for adventure, not misled by any primitivistic fallacy or lured by the luxury of vague revery, but because he believed that "man is a part and parcel of Nature rather than a member of society." In the pungent expression of his convictions and experiences he "nailed worlds to their primitive senses" and "transplanted" them to his page with the earth which he loved so intensely adhering to their roots. Extreme certainly in his disdain for society, in his devotion to nature, and in his eccentric aloofness, Thoreau differs from most romanticists in his calm stability. He was not given to "causes" of any kind. There is so much of the realist, the universal and timeless in him that one hesitates to label him at all except as "bachelor of nature."

Between Longfellow and the Transcendental group Whittier occupies a middle ground. In his Quaker dependence upon the "inner light" he belongs obviously to the latter, while as a genial balladist of New England life and of older times he rivals the Cambridge poet. Yet deriving his first creative inspiration from Burns, who taught him to see

> through all familiar things
> The romance underlying,

he was by the circumstances of his life able to celebrate more intimately and completely than a college professor the scenes of humble life. Far more intensely than the Transcendentalists, on the other hand, he flamed in noble ire against the evil of slavery. In his own words, he was

> a dreamer born,
> Who with a mission to fulfil,
> Had left the Muses' haunts to turn
> The crank of an opinion-mill.

Out of the opinion-mill, however, came much of the expression of his intense faith in equality and in the dignity of labor. In his simplicity and childlike convictions Whittier was a great social romanticist.

The poetic energy not only of Whittier but of other Northern writers was evoked by the growing menace of slavery. In fact the strange anomaly of negro bondage in the first democratic state became the motive force of a humanitarian protest which may be called the second wave of the romantic movement in the social realm, and which gathered intensity second only to the original agitation for human rights in the eighteenth century. Abolition and the frontier perhaps constitute America's most distinctive contribution to the progress of romanticism. Yet apart from the slavery issue the chief American writers before the Civil War were astonishingly oblivious to the turbulent and bewildering expansion of the nation on all frontiers, geographical, political, industrial. Emerson and Thoreau did catch the thrill of this new civilization suddenly spreading over the whole continent, and they reflected their vision in occasional memorable passages. But their feeling of kinship with the masses who were creating this crude, eagerly acquisitive society was limited to the small farmers about Concord. They could not become intoxicated merely by crossing Brooklyn ferry, "one of that centripetal and centrifugal gang." They could only point the way to one "turbulent, fleshly, sensual, eating,

drinking, and breeding," and when he arrived, exclaim,
"Unto us a man is born!"

I am of old and young, of the foolish as much as the wise,
    . . . a child as well as a man,
Stuff'd with the stuff that is coarse and stuff'd with the
    stuff that is fine, . . .
A Southerner soon as a Northerner, . . .
A Kentuckian walking the vale of the Elkhorn in my deer-
    skin leggings, a Louisianian or Georgian,
A boatman over lakes or bays or along coasts, a Hoosier,
    Badger, Buckeye; . . .
Comrade of Californians, comrade of free North-Westerners,
    (loving their big proportions) . . .
Of every hue and caste am I, of every rank and religion,
A farmer, mechanic, artist, gentleman, sailor, quaker,
Prisoner, fancy-man, rowdy, lawyer, physician, priest.

This is the meaning of Walt Whitman. No one ever
reached out and embraced the whole, good and bad,
coarse and fine, with such universal enthusiasm. In him
culminated more completely than in any other American all the elements of romanticism. But he transcends
previous expression of these elements with prodigal
originality. Equality took on new and startling literal-
ness in his mind; democracy became mystic and even
cosmic in its significance; the academic doctrine of
brotherhood proclaimed in rhapsodic accent as incar-

nate in the very tides of American life. So entirely committed was he to the independent destiny of his country that he dared to repudiate even Shakespeare as narrowly aristocratic and carried out to extreme (we can hardly say logical) conclusion Emerson's plea for a new American literature in his contention for novel literary forms. His own innovations in unrimed, endlessly enumerative style undeniably expressive of the teeming life of the nation (we need not explain) not only inaugurated a new movement in poetry but emphasized the realistic and naturalistic tendencies developing out of certain aspects of romanticism.

So much of a comprehensive sketch has been useful, I hope, in assembling the facts, which are familiar enough, but which hitherto have not been isolated and rearranged in the present pattern. Thus presented in brief survey, one or more elements of romanticism stand out pervasively in the work of each of the principal writers. Colonial romanticism begins in the perception of vision of "a new man who acts upon new principles," possible only amid the unique opportunities of the New World. During the Revolution and in the earliest years of the nation these new principles become more definitely and independently formulated as the confession of faith of a new society. Only in a general sense were they derived from the Old World. It was America which showed the way not only in applying but in shaping visions of political and social individualism.

In the first stages, then, American romanticism was as independent as English, French, or German. During the following decades our literature naturally absorbed ideas, impulses, forms, from current English writing. But some it simulated and reproduced in both derivative and original fashion; others it rejected. Romance in the older sense it fed upon with eagerness, reproducing romance themes in fiction and drama, but also reflecting distinctively American scenes in romantic manner. Of the new romanticism the various elements reappear sometimes in derivative, often in more original forms modified by the American environment. Revolt against tradition and authority takes the form of asserting national independence in social and political, but not in literary or esthetic ideals. Until the present generation our literature shows extraordinarily little experiment in forms. Among other elements enumerated, the fresh perception of nature is pervasive, although often failing of memorable expression; the sense of wonder is rather surprisingly absent, seldom rising to the level of ecstasy; and in general our literature does not attain intensity in expression of the emotions and of imagination. The recovery of a more remote past as stimulus to emotional and imaginative outlooks is moreover comparatively unimportant. Far more characteristic is the reflection of humanitarian sympathies and the assertion of individual rights, though these are often implicit rather than explicit.

If the evidence appears somewhat negative, it is important to realize that our literature, although less romantic in degree, is prevailingly romantic in character. The romantic movement in America was wide in range and rich in achievement. But this general assertion and more specific critical contentions here made must be carefully tested. We need much detailed investigation of each aspect of romanticism and detailed final appraisals of the relative prevalence or absence of these aspects in each writer. We need also close comparisons between European and American romanticism. Only when such investigations are made can we formulate an intelligent critical estimate of American literary achievement during its most productive period.

# VII. THE DEVELOPMENT OF REALISM

## VERNON LOUIS PARRINGTON

THE historian of American realism is confronted with a complex and difficult theme that involves much more than a simple account of a new literary theory and practice. Back of every changing technique lies a changing philosophy, and back of a changing philosophy lie changing social ideals that in the end determine the national culture. In the late nineteenth century, it must be recalled, the mind of America was being subjected to a play of forces that brought into question the validity and excellence of the ideals hitherto predominant. For two generations the Industrial Revolution had been extending over an agrarian people the new sovereignty of the machine, and constraining a free individualism into conformity to a drab industrial pattern; and this revolutionary change, pregnant with future revolts, had gone forward briskly to the sound of romantic trumpets. Between 1815 and 1870, romanticism, economic even more than literary, had been the national religion. It had written a golden creed in terms of material expansion, of a buoyant and pervasive opti-

mism, to which every child of the *Zeitgeist* loyally sub-
scribed. It had dreamed vast dreams, and the hopes of its
Beriah Sellerses had been sustained by a childlike faith
in the pot of gold at the base of the rainbow. To question that faith or to doubt its sufficiency was a mark of
disloyalty that only a perverse fellow like Fenimore
Cooper was bold enough to subject himself to. So long
as the siren song of progress was in men's ears, America
would worship at the gaudy romantic altars and turn
away from a skeptical realism that proposed to examine
national ideals in the cold light of fact.

But with the early seventies came the first stirrings
of change. The gorgeous romantic soap-bubbles were
bursting on every hand. Disillusioned farmers and dis-
satisfied proletarians were beginning to question the
ways of capitalism, and from that questioning was
eventually to emerge a more realistic attitude towards
life and letters. Realism in America, it would appear,
rose out of the ashes of romantic faith. It sprang from
social discontent, and it came to maturity when that
discontent was clarified in the light of Old World
thought. European science and European social philosophy, augmented by European literary technique, com-
pleted the realistic revolution begun by the first disil-
lusionment with middle-class economics. There is
suggestion in the fact that the progressive phases of

realism in America have synchronized closely with the recurrent periods of economic depression that marked the development of an industrial order. The realism of Howells followed the panic of '73 and grew more serious with the labor disturbances of the late eighties; the realism of Garland emerged from the economic maladjustments that bred Populism; the realism of Crane and Norris came with the depression of the nineties; the realism of Herrick and Jack London coincided with the revolt of the Muckrakers that was strengthened by the depression of 1907; and the realism of Sinclair Lewis and Sherwood Anderson synchronized with the depression of post-war days. One must not make too much of such coincidences, yet it is clear at least that these successive probings of American life involved a criticism of current romantic ideals, and of the plutocracy that had gathered the pots of gold all were chasing.

But such probings of economic maladjustment were likely to find issue in sociological studies that might use the technique of realism while rejecting the philosophy of any adequate realistic theory. It was well-nigh impossible for the Victorian mind—the American Victorian, at least—to be realistic, as that term is understood today. It might set down objectively what lay before its eyes, but it was too deeply colored with the romantic philosophy of the Enlightenment, too confident in its teleological prepossessions, to envisage its materials with cool detachment and interpret them in the light of a realistic philosophy. The sociological novelist was a reformer, seeking particular ends, rather than a critical analyst of life; and not until the appearance of a generation familiar with the teachings of the laboratory did realism in America come of age.

Science must displace theology and metaphysics before that would come about. The intellectual history of the generation born after the Civil War is the history of the transition from Emerson to Herbert Spencer, and from Spencer to Ernst Haeckel—from Transcendentalism to biology, and from biology to physics—from the doctrine of the innate Godhood to the doctrine of biological perfectibility through evolution, and thence to the doctrine of a mechanistic cosmos that makes no account of teleological ends. From man as the first-born child of God, to man as a flea on the epidermis of earth, is a sufficiently revolutionary transition; yet once that transition had been made, the way was prepared for a mechanistic psychology that proposed to interpret the flea in terms of physiological structure and explain his activities as the consequence of glandular secretions. In presence of such philosophical materialisms the romantic optimism that suffused a genial glow over an egocentric universe, and the romantic freedom of the will that professed itself capable of shaping life to what ends it would, lost their sanctions and disintegrated, to be succeeded by a stark pessimism underlaid by a mechanistic determinism. The intellectual backgrounds were provided for a realism somber as that of the Russians, and Theodore Dreiser succeeded William Dean Howells and Hamlin Garland.

In the light of these two movements that cradled the young intellectuals of the last generation—concern at the social maladjustments resulting from the Industrial Revolution, and the encroachment of a mechanistic determinism upon the conception of evolutionary progress, with all teleological assumptions put away—it is possible to sketch the stages through which the developing movement of realism has passed in America. Overlapping somewhat and not quite continuous, the several stages are nevertheless suggestive: the realism of the commonplace in the work of Howells, which reached its culmination in the middle eighties; the realism of social protest in Garland's early work—1887-1893—which came to exuberant expression between 1903 and 1917; the realism of naturalism that began with Crane and Norris in the middle nineties and reached its fullest expression in the work of Dreiser; and the realism of impressionism—and perhaps expressionism—that began with *The Red Badge of Cour-*

*age* but has come into wide vogue only since the war. The work of Henry James I choose to exclude from the classification, for despite the accident of American birth James was culturally European and belongs to the history of English literature rather than to American.

Of these several phases much the most pervasive and domestic is the realism of social protest. It found its way into the pages of the *Atlantic*, as Professor Pattee has pointed out, so early as the sixties, and in the opening decade of the present century it swept pretty much all fiction into service to the social conscience. It was the protest largely of an older America against a younger; it embodied a phase of American experience worthy of intelligent and sympathetic study; but its main interest was social rather than literary. Its zeal for reform too often overweighed its love of fine craftsmanship and made it careless of a strict objectivity. An adequate bibliography is still wanting, but the movement contributed a huge list of novels from Twain and Warner's *The Gilded Age*, through Tourgee's *A Fool's Errand*, Henry Adams' *Democracy*, John Hay's *The Breadwinners*, Keenan's *The Moneymakers*, Marion Crawford's *An American Politician*, Boyesen's *The Golden Calf*, Fuller's *The Cliff-Dwellers*, Warner's *The Golden House*, Will Payne's *The Money Captain*, Robert Grant's *Unleavened Bread*, until with the new century it broad-

ened out into a roily engulfing stream. Immensely significant as the movement is to the student of American
*Kulturgeschichte*, it must be set apart from the narrower
realistic movement and regarded as primarily sociological, using the technique of realism to serve special ends.

With this underbrush cleared away, the field of realism emerges more clearly, and William Dean Howells,
with his elaborate transcriptions of the commonplace,
may be regarded as the first of our conscious and de-
liberate realists. The sources of his realism are somewhat
obscure. His quiet technique has been variously traced
to Jane Austen, to the drab pages of Eggleston's *Hoosier
Schoolmaster*, even to the realistic humor of the frontier
from Gus Longstreet to the Pike school. But all such attempts are a little futile, and we can probably do no
better than consider Howells' own analysis of the
sources of realism and deduce his technique from them.
In *Criticism and Fiction*, which is a late summary and
defense of a faith he had long held, he traces realism
to the twin sources of science and democracy. "Realism,"
he says, "is nothing more and nothing less than the
truthful treatment of material"; and the sole criterion
he sets up is objective reality. "We must ask ourselves
before we ask anything else, Is it true?—true to the
motives, the impulses, the principles that shape the life
of actual men and women?" From the second source,

democracy, it derives its all-embracing sympathy that finds nothing mean or commonplace when rightly understood, and will hold no commerce with the spirit of aristocratic aloofness. The spirit of aristocracy, Howells was fond of pointing out, driven in from its outer defenses, has taken refuge in romanticism. The pride of caste has become the pride of taste; and it is this final citadel that realism is laying siege to. Democracy has taught the great lesson of the essential dignity of all life, and the realist, because he is a democrat, "feels in every nerve the equality of things and the unity of men." In this faith Howells accepts the Emersonian creed, "I ask not the great, the remote, the romantic. . . . I embrace the common; I sit at the feet of the familiar and the low."

Thus interpreted, the realism of Howells—in its second great impulse at least—is revealed as a native attitude, an expression of the national faith coming at last to flower in literature. It is a final expression of the broad democratic movement that in his youth was shaping American ideals in harmony with the philosophy of the Enlightenment, that had been reflected in the idealism of Emerson and Thoreau, and had come to romantic expression in the formless enthusiasms of Whitman. By his own quiet path the young Howells came to the same buoyant faith; and if his "gay American horizons" were cloudless, if for him "the more pleasing aspects of life" were the more American, the fact suggests that he also was a child of the Enlightenment. Science had not knocked at his door to disturb his simple faith, and the Industrial Revolution had not yet destroyed the genial optimism in which that faith had been nurtured. For years he refused to immerse himself in the turbid stream of his generation. He was a bookman, and he dwelt apart from the fierce scramble that was destroying the America of the Enlightenment—first at Venice as a reverent pilgrim to Italian shrines, later at Cambridge as a reverent pilgrim to Brahmin shrines. The vulgarities of the Gilded Age passed him by. Immersed in culture, his democracy bleached out into a kindly and generous faith in the excellence of life in America and the nobility of commonplace men and women. It was during these years that his realism took form, and he set himself to depict the society in which he moved—Cambridge and Boston of the Age of Innocence, where women held sway and a maidenly reticence was reckoned the crown of womanhood. And so as a realist Howells became a specialist in women's nerves, a prober of the New England conscience troubled by invisible cobwebs, a master of Beacon Street small-talk, a portrayer of impeccable Back Bay manners. It was this world that shaped his refined technique and provided

the stuff of such works as *The Rise of Silas Lapham,*
*April Hopes,* and *Indian Summer*—leisurely studies with
a lambent humor that plays about the edges of his talk
and gives flavor to pages that otherwise must have been
insipid.

But with his discovery of the Russians and his removal to New York in 1889, a change came over his
mind. The earlier Howells did not survive the removal.
The brutal realities of the great city struck across his
social conscience. The bitter unrest with its Haymarket
Riot, its Knights of Labor, its strikes and lockouts, was
an eloquent commentary on the teachings of Tolstoy.
The gates of the Age of Innocence were closing behind
him, and a different Howells emerged in *A Hazard of*
*New Fortunes* and *A Traveller from Altruria*—a Howells who had turned radical and accepted a Socialist key
to the riddle of social justice. In a younger man this
darkening of his gay horizons, this realization that the
buoyancy of Emersonian democracy consorted ill with a
brutal and rapacious plutocracy, must have produced a
revolutionary overturn in his art; but he had too long
practiced his leisurely craft to adopt a new technique,
and the literary aftermath of this late awakening of his
social conscience was a criticism of industrial America
done with such gentle urbanity as to throw a veil over
the black depths he was exploring and conceal from his

readers the significance of his revelations. He could not convey to others the gloom of the horizons that were darkening for him. The realism of the commonplace was inadequate to carry the new burden of meaning, yet it was too late to learn a different technique, and Howells remained a Victorian, immersed in discursive pages, long after he must have known that his realism was becoming obsolete.

To Hamlin Garland, however, just entering on an apprenticeship to his craft, such bright glancings over the surface of life seemed like a shirking of the artist's duty. The shadows did not lurk in the background for him; they were obscuring his sun and he must speak out bluntly. He must strip away the veil of urbanity and summon all America to peer into the black depths with him. And so in the hands of this earnest and humorless young man realism became trenchant and severe, concerned with the soil and sweat of drab and laborious days. Life was too exigent for him to indulge in genial commonplaces. The Middle Border of his experience was a land over which brooded the shadow of tragedy. The buoyant optimism of pioneer days was gone from the prairies, and a fierce resentment had taken its place. And this resentment, stirring amongst the sons of Jacksonians, aroused a distrust of capitalism that was using government to exploit the farmers. Garland was a stern Puritan idealist, disciplined by adversity. His youth was passed in an environment that was sowing the seeds of rebellion in the heart of the prairie pioneer, and he quitted that world in the hope of discovering a more generous way of life than was possible on an Iowa homestead. In his fierce quest of knowledge he found excellent masters—Taine, Spencer, Whitman, Henry George, William Morris; and from their pages he got a militant philosophy that was to set his pen to work. It was while brooding over their teachings, in the poverty-stricken Boston days, alone and groping, that he wrote his first sketches of the Middle Border—harsh and acrid pages from his own life which were to grow into *Main-Travelled Roads*.

That was in 1887. In the same year other beginnings of a disillusioned realism of farm life were being made— by Harold Frederic in *Seth's Brother's Wife*, and by Joseph Kirkland in *Zury, The Meanest Man in Spring County*. But Garland was the first "dirt farmer" to write of farm life, and he was conscious of undertaking pioneer work. In the next few years he pondered much over the function of art and came to conclusions embodied later in *Crumbling Idols*: that art is individual, that it must tell the truth as the artist sees is, that it must serve society. From his conception of creative individualism came a justification of the local color school, and from his theory of social service came his interest in causes that sets his stories so sharply apart from the work of the naturalists. His dissatisfaction with the surface realism of Howells was intensified by two influences that came into his life during these early years—Henry George and B. O. Flower; and under their guidance his art turned away to serve the cause of Single Tax and the diverse radicalisms gathered under the banner of Populism. His deep loyalty to the Middle Border impelled him to join in its great crusade, and he took up his pen with an earnest conviction of the justice of the agrarian cause. During the stirring years of the ferment he poured out a stream of books, three of which—*Main-Travelled Roads, Prairie Folks*, and *Rose of Dutcher's Coolly*—in their searching truthfulness reached a height of mordant realism he never afterwards attained. Other studies of those early years—*Jason Edwards, A Spoil of Office*, and *A Member of the Third House*—were vigorous bits of propaganda that have been forgotten with the causes they served.

After the subsidence of the ferment Garland put away his realism and turned to the romance that had been the Promised Land of his starved youth. A confirmed realist, with a single-hearted devotion to objective presentation, he seems never to have been. His theory of fidelity to the *milieu*, indeed, would seem to

cut deeper and reveal more of his art than the conception
of fidelity to the technique of realism. Perhaps at bot-
tom they are the same; be that as it may, some justification can be urged in defense of his later work. As he
shifted his *milieu* and the light changed on his landscape, fidelity to local color would work a change in
his palette. He was born a dozen years too soon to feel
the full impact of the Industrial Revolution and the
scientific revolution on a mind still plastic; and so while
Dreiser was being molded by those revolutions he turned
away to new fields. At heart he was a romantic, with a
longing for a beautiful life, and when the reaction came
he sought the "wide free spaces" in the mountain land
beyond the Middle Border—a land where his imagination might range freely, untrammeled by sordid petti-
ness. Yet even there he found causes to appeal to his
sensitive social conscience. *The Captain of the Gray
Horse Troop* is a plea for the Indians who were being
despoiled by the herders and the politicians; it is vigorous work, but it is not in the vein of his earlier
realism. His work in that field was pretty much done.
*Moccasin Ranch* (1909) with its bleak Dakota background and its suggestion of a mechanistic universe, and
*A Son of the Middle Border,* with its idyllic atmosphere,
are notable studies, but *Main-Travelled Roads* remains
his great contribution to American realism.

A child of the passionate agrarian upheaval, Garland belonged to a world that was passing. The years of the nineties were resentful and bitter, convulsed by the great struggle between an older America and a younger. In that struggle the naïve individualism that had been the bequest of the romantic revolution went down in defeat; the ideals of a triumphant plutocracy superseded the ideals of a decentralized agrarian society; and the philosophy of the Enlightenment was quietly put away. That life is good, that human nature is excellent, that man's fate can be molded like the potter's clay, that democratic progress is the law of evolution—these conceptions no longer seemed so self-evident as they had seemed to an earlier generation. In the early nineties the shadows were again falling across the American mind. A tyrannical social complexity, with its industrial city and its mass psychology, was in the way of creating a new caste regimentation, more hopeless than that from which our ancestors had fled three centuries before and from which they had found release in the freedoms of an unpeopled continent. A pessimistic determinism, rising out of the imperious drift of social forces, lay dark on the American horizons; and this evil specter, not unlike the harsh Calvinistic dogma, was sanctioned by the vision of a cosmos bleak, impersonal, obeying only physical forces, discovered in the philosophy of Ernst

Haeckel. The old teleological foundations of American optimism were disintegrating, and the intellectual backgrounds were preparing from which was to emerge a realism amoral, deterministic, dark with pessimism. The American novelist was at last in a mood to understand, as Howells and Garland could not, the significance of French and Russian naturalism. Flaubert and Zola, Tolstoy and Turgeniev, were finally to set their imprint on our realism, for the reason that American experience had created the *milieu* in which a similar realism was inevitable.

From such a background emerged in the nineties three writers, Stephen Crane, Frank Norris, and Theodore Dreiser, who were to create for America the type of realism to which Zola had given the name naturalism. It was impersonal and objective, but it was very much more than that; it was equipped with a philosophy got from the physical sciences. It conceived of man as a complex of physical drives, dwelling in a mechanistic world, caught and destroyed in a web of internal and external forces. The new realism was brilliantly begun with *Maggie, A Girl of the Streets,* written in 1891-1893, when Crane was only twenty, a "bit of episodic slum fiction" that portrayed a world without virtues held in the grip of herd taboos; and it was continued by Norris's *McTeague,* written in 1894-1899, an analysis of low-grade characters destroyed by an ironical fate, and by *Vandover and the Brute,* written in 1894-1914, a grim study in character degeneration. But Crane and Norris were not destined to carry far the work thus brilliantly begun. After a great popular success with *The Red Badge of Courage*—an early study in impressionism—Crane soon succumbed to ill health; and Norris, influenced by Zola's sociological canvases, turned away in *The Octopus* to paint a vast Zolaesque *milieu,* yielded to an innate romanticism of temper, and never again rose to the high plane of *McTeague.* The work of carrying on the movement of naturalism fell to Dreiser, in whose successive full-length studies of American figures the twin revolutionary forces of the times came to completest expression. On this German peasant the impact of the Industrial Revolution and the scientific revolution struck with devastating effect, sweeping away the old faith in a free individualism in a benevolent universe, and substituting a bleak mechanistic philosophy. Sociological in method, he has remained objective, detached, amoral, never concerned with reform, skeptical of all Utopian enthusiasms, dealing veraciously with "that animal called man," and feeling for him a vast pity.

After its promising beginning the movement of naturalism, unfortunately, was cut across, first by a sporadic outburst of romanticism that from 1898 to 1903 yielded

a roily flood of historical fiction, and second by the
Muckraking movement that from 1903 to the outbreak
of the War drew pretty much all literature into its
orbit. The mass of output during those years of a
rising liberalism is not easily reduced to order; yet
certain characteristics emerge with sufficient sharpness.
It was sociological in theme, in the earlier years political—an expression of the Progressive movement in politics—and in the later years economic—an expression of
the economic interpretation of history, then rising into
popular consciousness; and its purpose was to instruct
the American middle class in the intimate relationship
between economics and politics. In part it was wholly
native, the protest of the traditional democratic faith
that hated plutocracy and proposed to cut its claws by
new democratic scissors; and in part it was European,
an attempt to domesticate in America the teachings of
Marxian socialists. Broadly speaking, the political novelists, writers like Winston Churchill, William Allen
White, and Booth Tarkington, were romantics of the
old school of the Enlightenment who wore the garb of
realism somewhat awkwardly; whereas the economic
novelists, writers like Robert Herrick, Upton Sinclair,
Jack London, and Ernest Poole, were Marxians who had
learned their realism in the school of economic rather
than scientific determinism.

Of the multitude of novelists that belong to the movement, Herrick and London must serve for examples, and in their intellectual attitudes are revealed the same influences that created the naturalism of Dreiser. Both were hostile to the machine civilization created by the Industrial Revolution, and both were influenced by the mechanistic interpretations of science; yet there persisted in them something of the Marxian faith that the determinism of historical evolution is on the side of social justice, and that out of the class war will come eventually a proletarian commonwealth wherein all shall share the good things of life. In that faith, more hopeful than the bleak Dreiserian creed, they enlisted for the Revolution, and their successive stories were scenes from the social struggle that is preparing the future. They were the completest expression of the hopes of those vigorous years when liberalism was passing over into radicalism, before all social faith was destroyed by the war. Of these documents, so soon to grow old-fashioned, Herrick's *Memoirs of an American Citizen,* with its background of the Haymarket Riot and its suggestion of the Nietzschean basis of business ethics, and London's *Martin Eden,* with its background of science and its scornful rejection of bourgeois values, will serve to suggest the affinities between sociological studies and realism. The method is realistic; yet in neither is the temper naturalistic, and they are dwarfed by Dreiser's colossal figure of Frank Cowperwood that in its simple objectivity is the greatest figure drawn by the earlier realists.

The great movement of liberalism—the greatest since the golden forties—was brought to a rude end by the War, and when that fruitless adventure was over, the sociological novel was as old-fashioned as faith in Jacksonian democracy. In the cynical post-war days the will to power had become the law of a mechanistic civilization, and frustrated idealists turned upon that civilization with savage scorn. Realism, bitter and disillusioned, was the common mood, and it threw upon men and war and civilization the light of its disillusion. Determinism no longer wore a benevolent Marxian aspect, discovering in every revolution a potential Utopia; it had again become grim, sordid, amoral, pessimistic. The ways of civilization were in for a searching scrutiny. In the bestiality of trench warfare naturalism discovered a fitting theme, and the war books uncovered a brutal realism unknown before in America. The futilities of our middle-class life provoked the biting satire of *Main Street* and *Babbitt* and the drab realism of *Miss Lulu Bett* and *The Narrow House*. But the deeper drift of realism was towards a crisp objective impressionism that painted the forms and colors of reality; and an inquisitive expressionism that probed the mysterious inner experience of men and women—a life shut up in the skull-pan like a Chinese prisoner in his iron-bound coffin, with only narrow apertures through which to communicate with the external world. The realist has become a psychologist, a neo-Freudian concerned with inner drives and the furtive subconscious life. Sherwood Anderson in his self-obsession is as sturdy a rebel against industrialism as Dreiser, but he has discovered the great obstacle to human happiness in the mechanism of man. Life is a trap, but the trap is planted deep in human instincts, and the search for the "white wonder" brings the jaws together. *The Triumph of the Egg* is a very different sort of realism from the realism practiced by Mr. Howells, and it serves to measure the distance American experience has traveled in a single generation. The prude and the blue-stocking have been consigned to the garret. The last shred of Victorian reticence has been stripped away, and the animal called man stands before us naked and unashamed—in poetry and the drama, as well as in fiction. America, we like to say, is coming of age.

# VIII. AMERICAN HISTORY AND AMERICAN LITERARY HISTORY

## A. M. SCHLESINGER

"WE are now ready," says Professor Foerster of his co-workers in American literary history, "for free and fresh thought, for scientific thought, for the undisturbed use of observation, reason, and imagination." Advice from an onlooker is usually free, often decidedly fresh, and too frequently based on an undisturbed use of observation compounded with imagination rather than reason. Allowances should therefore be made for the lucubrations of the present writer, who is by training a student of American social history rather than of the history of American letters. Yet the conviction generally expressed by the contributors to this volume of the desirability of a closer *entente* between workers in the two fields may perhaps secure a lenient hearing for observations that might otherwise seem less pertinent than impertinent.

What first impresses the social historian is that his fellow delver in the literary field has been mainly interested in the picturesque, the unusual, and the super-excellent. The same preoccupation, it is well to recall, was the dominant complex of the historian himself a generation ago. He surveyed the past through lenses that revealed only mountain peaks, majestic vistas, and extinct craters; the stream of history swirled about great heroes, epical battles, and imposing institutions. But no self-respecting historical student today believes that the topography of history consists of a few glittering land-marks, or, for that matter, that the landmarks can be accurately determined without a thorough knowledge of the terrain of which they form a part. The point of view has changed from the heavens above to the earth below. It is now recognized that many of the mighty movements that have affected the destiny of man had their origins in obscure places; they gathered strength in hidden valleys and along dusty highways, and were carried through to success by the united efforts of hordes of nameless men and women. Moreover the historian's scale of values has materially altered as his test of the significance of an historical event has changed from that of the welfare of an aristocracy or ruling class to that of the well-being of the multitude.

There have been signs in the last ten years that re-search in American literary history is taking a similar turn. Whether or not these occasional enterprises repre-sent a genuine change of heart, it is safe to predict that sooner or later the student in that field will have to quit the easy practice of picking out the little bits that interest him and undertake the task of bringing the whole complex bewildering picture into focus. This approach involves, of course, something vastly more than an acquaintance with polite letters, indeed nothing less than an intimate knowledge of the writings, good, bad, and indifferent, in which the mass of men have found instruction, inspiration, amusement, and escape. Historically, and to every one but the literary critic, the chief significance of the printed word arises from its use as a medium of communication among human beings, horizontally in its application to contemporary society, vertically as applied to the transmission of knowledge from generation to generation.

This, it is clear, is an approach to letters as one of the social sciences. The objective becomes an understanding of the literary culture of a people—their culture as embodied in print—in all its aspects, but with the main attention always fixed on what is broadly diffused rather than on what is unusual or special. Writing from this point of view, no historian of American letters, however highly he might personally esteem Ralph Waldo Emerson, could treat the middle third of the nineteenth century without devoting considerably more space to the activities of William H. McGuffey, whose school readers, widely used through a space of sixty years, did more to influence the general literary tastes and standards of the period than the soft effulgent rays of the entire Cambridge-Concord constellation. Even in this year of Our Lord there are more McGuffey clubs in the United States than Browning societies; and only a few years ago a devout McGuffeyite could write in a Boston paper—Boston!—

> Scholastic bee, fastidious,
>     Who gathered patiently for us
> The nectar from a thousand sources
>     Of flowery lore and ripe discourses:
> A taste of Shakespeare and of Poe,
>     Of Scott and Harriet Beecher Stowe,
> Assorted well and expurgated,
>     With dots and stars interpolated—
> Perhaps his tomes were somewhat stuffy,
>     But I revere the name McGuffey.

No one is disposed to question the important service which the esthetic critic renders to the study of letters, even though his dicta are usually rated higher by his contemporaries than by posterity. Undoubtedly, too, his criteria are often useful to the literary historian in arranging and classifying his materials. It remains, however, that literary criticism and literary history are two distinct branches of scholarship, each with its own point of view and technique, and having no more in common than, say, history in general and the study of ethics. Until the historian of letters frees himself from the domination of the literary critic, his work is certain to fall short of its highest promise.

If American literary history needs to be studied from a broadly social point of view, it is only shifting the emphasis a little to regard it as being, in a very special sense, a branch of *Kulturgeschichte*. Letters form merely one channel through which the creative and imaginative energies of man seek outlet, often not the most important one. To understand the literary trends of a period it thus becomes necessary to study and compare the forces at work in other cultural fields: the old geocentric attitude toward literature must yield to a more comprehensive view.

Consider the first half century after 1776, a period whose key the social historian finds in the determination to achieve cultural independence in the same sense that the founders of the nation had won political independence. This audacious effort was in many cases premature, and its results sometimes grotesque; but it was a necessary preparation of the national mind for the clear, pure note of Emerson a little later, and certain of its accomplishments were of enduring importance. In religion this spirit showed itself in the withdrawal of

American denominations from their European connections, the temporary setback of the pro-English Episcopalians and Methodists, the substantial progress toward the establishment of freedom of worship and church equality, the first stirrings of Unitarianism and Universalism. In the domain of law it caused courts and legislatures to repudiate the English common law; it introduced greater humanity into the penal code and brought about the destruction of those props of English aristocratic society: primogeniture and entail. It was further responsible for the adoption of the practice of compiling American court decisions as the basis of an autochthonous legal system. In the educational realm it led to the founding of the first state universities and produced an ardent agitation, assisted by President Washington and his successors, for the establishment of a national university. In the field of government the class-bound conservatism of Hamilton and his school—who thought the British form of government "the best in the world" and the Constitution "only a stepping-stone to something better"—was mellowed into the democratic liberalism and tolerance of the Jeffersonian Republicans.

Not less strong was the urge to nationalism in the fine arts. In painting the portraitists turned rapturously to limning the likenesses of American heroes (Charles Willson Peale executed fourteen pictures of Washington, Gilbert Stuart nearly forty); and their exertions were presently paralleled by the zealous application of a group of landscapists—the Hudson River School—to the novel and patriotic task of preserving on canvas glimpses of American scenery. Architecture was a more difficult matter; but even here it was at least possible to reject the old English tradition, and adopt in its stead a mode more fitting the stern republican virtues of the new nation, that of classical Rome—a decision, by the way, which scattered handsome colonnaded mansions over the Southern countryside and set the mold for hundreds of state capitals and county courthouses. In American music the chief significance of the period arises from the fact that it produced three of our great national anthems: "Hail Columbia," "The Star-Spangled Banner," and "America." Even the science of healing had its "American system of medicine," devised and practiced by Benjamin Rush and other physicians who had been trained on the battlefields of the Revolution.

Approached from this background, the varied literary developments of the period, ranging from nursery rimes through fiction and poetry to Webster's epoch-making dictionary, take on new meaning and significance. At first sight it seems only a matter for mirth that Samuel Latham Mitchill, a foremost scientist and

medico of New York, should have proposed to revise
"Four and twenty blackbirds" so as to read:

> When the pie was opened,
> The birds they were songless,
> Was not that a pretty dish
> To set before the Congress?

"While I discard the King of England," the good man
explained, "with whom we have nothing to do, I give
them [the children] some knowledge of our general
government by specifying our Congress." Yet he was
moved by precisely the same pride of nationality that
animated the efforts of the jurists, musicians, legislators,
and the rest, and that inspired Noah Webster to undertake his series of enterprises for improving and codify-
ing American orthography and grammar.

Indeed, Webster was the greatest intellectual force in
the American literary culture of the era; and far from
being the dry-as-dust pedant that he is usually pictured,
he was a robust nationalist whose influence on the form
and spirit of American letters has been as great as that
of his illustrious namesake on the spirit of American
government. In his first systematic treatise on grammar
(1783) he declared, envisaging a glorious future for
American literature, "For America in her infancy to

adopt the present maxims of the Old World would be to stamp the wrinkle of decrepit old age upon the bloom of youth, and to plant the seed of decay in a vigorous constitution"; and nearly half a century later (1828) he introduced his monumental *American Dictionary of the English Language* with the prediction: "In fifty years from this time the American-English will be spoken by more people than all the dialects of the language; and in one hundred and thirty years by more people than any other language on the globe." Meantime he had performed doughty service in simplifying and standardizing English spelling, accomplishing among other things the important result of bringing that puzzling art within the reach of the common man.

The practitioners of imaginative and expository writing were quite as deeply affected by the spirit of the age. If there was a Hudson River School among the artists, there was something very like it among the romancers. This is to be seen most clearly in Irving, who, as has often been pointed out, defied a well-established literary convention when he found materials for legend and romance in the very river which the painters sought to celebrate. If a cult of hero worship obtained among the portraitists, there was a much more pernicious form of idolatry practiced by the historical writers, of whom Parson Weems, inventor of the cherry-tree myth, will remain the unforgettable example. If the song writers could find inspiration only in heroic national memories, Charles Brockden Brown and James Fenimore Cooper emulated them in a measure when they boldly chose the incidents and settings of their novels from the historical experiences of the American people. In a similar manner the stage was cluttered with home-made melodramas based on obvious patriotic themes and destined quickly to be forgotten by a critical posterity. Should works like these be dismissed as being merely popular and thus of negligible importance, it remains that the chief belletristic writers of the period were of the same mind. The ponderous offgivings of the Hartford Wits, more admired than read even at the time, represented a brave attempt to create a national epic literature. On the whole their endeavors have escaped oblivion hardly better than those of the playwrights.

It matters little that the literary culture of the first half century of Independence remained essentially European and imitative; after all, the writers could humanly do no more than attempt here and there to stem the flood of ideas, fashions, and literary standards which poured in on them from the maturer civilizations of the Old World. Nevertheless, something of great spiritual importance had been accomplished. The workers in all

cultural fields thrilled with a sense of national consciousness that has formed a continuing incentive to achievement ever since. A similar unity of social, intellectual,
and spiritual life exists in every other stage of American
development, and indeed might be even more convinc-
ingly set forth, for example, as respects the period after
1825, when the central interest was the rise of the plain
people and human perfectibility was a creed. It is clear
that the conventional periodization of American literary history needs thorough reconsideration. The old
boundaries, settled on purely bookish principles and
from a partial view, will have to be reëstablished in the
light of a broader and more realistic understanding of
all the factors involved.

Closely related to this conception of the parallelism
of cultural phenomena is the conception of their inter-
action and interdependence. The student of literature is
under a constant temptation to keep his eyes so close
to the particular specimen under examination that, like
the old-time botanist observing a blossom under a
microscope, he often forgets that the plant has roots, a
stem, a system of life, and is affected by changes in
temperature, soil, and other incidental conditions. The
product of such efforts is frequently hardly better than
a genealogy of printed works, one book begetting an-

other—literature studied in a vacuum, without relation to anything but itself.

It is true, of course, that books do beget books, that Emerson, for instance, was deeply indebted to Kant, and that Scott and Cooper were the literary progenitors of Simms and John Esten Cooke. But to stop at this point is to miss some of the most important influences that have shaped American letters. The literary historian of the future will have to widen his vision and take into proper account such factors as the invention of the rotary press, the state of general education and enlightenment, the constant cheapening of the processes of printing, the increasing ease of travel and communication, the distribution of surplus wealth and leisure, the introduction of the typewriter, the distribution of bookstores and circulating libraries, the popularization of the telephone, motor car, movie, and radio, and legislative attitudes toward such questions as censorship, international copyright, and a tariff on foreign books.

Nor are factors like these incapable of analysis and clarification. Take the spread of public schools in the generation before the Civil War, a subject to which the admirable and encyclopedic *Cambridge History of American Literature* devotes but a brief section and in it completely ignores the possibility of any vital relation between the new education and literary production.

From about 1825 to 1850 the great battle over the governmental support and direction of schooling was fought throughout the North and West; and by the latter date, if not before, most people in those sections enjoyed the privilege of receiving, without charge, instruction of at least an elementary sort. The ability to read and write ceased to be a special perquisite of the upper classes and became a possession of the multitude.

The effect on literary activity was unprecedented, comparable only to the invention of movable-type printing in the middle of the fifteenth century. For the first time it became worth while to write for a wide circle of readers; for the first time, in America at least, thousands of persons hitherto mute suddenly found themselves vocal. To put it differently, in the course of a short generation there emerged the most numerous reading public the world had ever known. The results were far-reaching in America both for good and evil. Its repercussions were felt even across the waters, where British authors found their potential audience many times enlarged, and, though denied the full profits of their labors by the lack of international copyright protection, could nevertheless enjoy those internal revenues of the spirit which come from multiplied renown.

In the United States, Tom, Dick, and Harry in the thirties and forties hurried to express in print their whole gamut of yearnings, doubts, hopes, and fears, their adventures in intellectual discovery, their remedies for social ills, their preachments against wickedness. It was the most abundant outpouring the nation had ever known and a documentary revelation of the many-sided American mind such as exists for no earlier epoch. The *American Publishers' Circular* declared in 1855: "In no other country in the world is the condition and prospects of the book publisher so secure as in this"; and after referring to the zeal for reading of "our Milliners, Tailoresses and Chambermaids," concluded: "Whatever, in the shape of a book is printed here, will find a market if at all respectably meritorious." The truth of the writer's contention was visibly attested by the establishment of a succession of important publishing houses in the thirties and forties in New York, Boston, and Philadelphia, some of which survive to our own day. As conduits from these were the circulating libraries, which trebled in number between 1825 and 1850, and which, by making a single book available to many readers, carried the stream of literary culture to all sections of the population.

Perhaps most characteristic of all was the appearance of a vast and varied periodical literature. At the base of the pyramid was a new journalism, taking its manners, if not its morals, from the hustling and somewhat sensational "penny press," and bringing odd glimpses of the world into the humblest homes. At the peak perched a small group of belletristic magazines—the *Knicker-bocker, Dial, Southern Literary Messenger,* and the others—magazines of limited but rarefied circulation. In between was to be found virtually every type of periodical we know today: religious, scientific, technical, propagandist, professional, agricultural, feminine, juvenile, etc. Like called to like; information must be disseminated; causes must make converts. Lowell tells us, "Every possible form of intellectual and physical dyspepsia brought forth its gospel"; and apparently all reform groups believed that God is on the side of the heaviest vocabularies. Somewhat over seventy-five labor weeklies in many parts of the country began to be published during the period. Of temperance journals alone there were more than thirty weeklies and monthlies in the 1840's. Every religious denomination of any standing possessed a battery of periodicals representing its different activities and contending theologies. Children's magazines sprang up and multiplied, finding in the *Youth's Companion* (1827) apparently the secret of perpetual youth. Of "female" magazines over fifty have been discovered in the ante-bellum period, a fact which suggests to the social historian how little he yet knows of the place of women in the life of those years.

Evidences such as these form a fairly accurate quantitative gauge of the influence of the new mass education on literary productivity. Equally important, however, were the qualitative effects, though the subject is too large for more than brief mention here. The chief characteristic of the new reading public was the fact that it was only semi-literate, half-educated. Figures compiled by the United States Bureau of Education show, for example, that in 1840 the entire schooling obtained by the average American in his lifetime amounted to one year of two hundred days, in 1850 to a little more than two years, and even as late as 1870 to only about three and a half years. This does not mean, of course, that many men did not possess a college education, or that the average educational advantages of the New Englander, for instance, were not greater than those of the Southerner, or that individuals like Lincoln could not surmount the barriers of circumstance. Nevertheless it remained true that a writer who wished to appeal to a wide audience, thus garnering both profits and a reputation, must adapt his manner and matter to the tastes and intellectual capacity of a people whose book education had, for the most part, not gone beyond the level of the second or third grade. Such a public gazed with childlike wonder at the world that lived on the printed page, and asked of it only that it should not violate those homely precepts of moral worth which formed a part of their religious lore. They demanded Christlike heroes and heroines and satanic villains; they gagged at subtleties; and the poverty of their cultural experience made them place a premium on the sentimental and the romantic and on tales of adventure. Though a somewhat similar fashion prevailed abroad, we may assume that American literary culture would have been much as it was without the force of foreign example.

That the character of this reading public left its impress on American letters is observable at every level. Note the cheap newspaper press, with its first sentimental exploitation of police-court news; the vogue of the literary annuals and "parlor magazines," with their popularization of the *Charlotte Temple* type of romance; the tremendous moral effectiveness of such pious fictional tracts as *Ten Nights in a Barroom* and *Uncle Tom's Cabin;* the emergence of supersentimentalists like Mary J. Holmes, Augusta J. Evans, and Mrs. E. D. E. N. Southworth. Athens itself was not immune, for the managers of the Boston Public Library confessed in 1872 that the most popular authors of the day were Mary J. Holmes, Caroline Lee Hentz, and Mrs. Southworth. In humorous writing the genial byplay of Irving gave way to the coarser humor of an Artemus Ward and Orpheus C. Kerr, who found in phonetic spelling a sure appeal to the risibilities of a public which had itself just learned to spell correctly. The very appearance of the short story as a force in American fiction argued an audience incapable of the sustained attention which the full-length novel demands.

Even the gods in their heavens had feet of clay. Longfellow, with his simple moral teachings and his pleasing imagery, was read and greatly admired by his adult contemporaries, but it is significant that today he is known chiefly as the "children's poet." As for Hawthorne, his gifts of expression may well entitle him to rank with genius, but the pattern of moral conduct to which he adhered was precisely that of the writers in the "parlor magazines," and his most poignant preoccupation was with the suffering and remorse which tormented those who rebelled against the accepted code. Traces of a similar sentimentality may be found in Poe—in "William Wilson," for instance—but, in general, Poe escaped the cramping restrictions of the period by projecting his characters into other times and "wild weird climes." He suffered the penalty of failing to obtain contemporary appreciation at home, though he insured for himself a wider fame. In a different sense much the same thing was true of the mystic who communed with the stars at Concord. While receptive to other influences of his day, Emerson gave little heed to the special limitation: of the reading public. The public in turn declined to buy his books, although, puzzled and stirred by something in the man himself, they were willing to pay to hear his living voice from the lyceum platform.

The story of ante-bellum literature cannot be told solely in terms of the state of education of the masses. Other factors, of course, need to be taken into account, such as the mechanical improvements in printing, the frontier influence, and the deeply religious tone of society. But the inclusion of these elements would only serve to reënforce the main contention, namely, that the development of literature is constantly affected by the forces which condition the whole course of social growth. American literary history has as yet received little attention from this point of view. In no aspect of the subject are useful results more certain of attainment, and perhaps nowhere else will the literary student and the social historian find coöperation more fruitful.

The emphasis which this paper has placed on broad trends and general points of view is due to no failure to appreciate the rôle which the elusive human personality plays in literature. It would be folly to maintain that an author's work can be completely understood from a knowledge of the culture pattern or patterns in which he has been entangled. But the biographical approach to letters carries one somewhat afield from the confines of social history. It involves not only a thorough mastery of the social and intellectual background but, in addition, a working familiarity with the essentials of biology, medicine, the several schools of psychology, and perhaps other sciences.

The emotional content of literature is so important, for instance, that it would seem imprudent for the student interested in the inner motivation of authorship to ignore the experimental evidence, collected by Cannon, Crile, Kempf, and others, which shows that the emotions are directly and indirectly controlled by the glands of internal secretion. Berman, indeed, goes so far as to say that "without thyroid no thought, no growth, no distinctive humanity or even animality is possible." Psychoanalysis, with its prepossession for hidden urges and unconscious impulses, already counts an increasing number of literary biographers among its followers, though the temptation to easy generalization into which some of them have fallen has yielded results so grotesque that serious students have been antagonized.

In exploring these twilight zones of interpretation the social historian can be of little help, since he is in much the same plight as the literary chronicler. In most cases, of course, it is clear that full medical and psychological data in regard to men and women of the past are not to be secured. It is further baffling to discover that on many points the scientists themselves are in disagreement. Yet the new knowledges and hypotheses of human personality and motivation are rich with suggestion for the discerning student, and he cannot wisely close his eyes to them. Either he must employ the traditional, unconvincing, rule-of-thumb diagnoses that have been the stock-in-trade of biographers from time immemorial, or, if he prefer a less fantastic course, he will avail himself of such guidance as modern science has to offer.

# IX.  AMERICAN LITERARY HISTORY AND AMERICAN LITERATURE

## HARRY HAYDEN CLARK

SUMMING up the problem of American literature,
Professor Foerster says, "*All* the factors may be
comprised under two heads: European culture and the
American environment." The foregoing essays have
treated various aspects of these two factors, and have
made clear the emphasis which is today being laid upon
background of one sort or another. It is perhaps time
to rest for a moment from analysis and contemplate a
synthesis: How is all the new material which investigation has provided to be focused upon our major literature? How is the picture of American literature to be
given perspective once more? What are the net results
to be? Is there danger of losing sight of the foreground
in our sweeping contemplation of background? From
the older extreme of considering isolated American
books "in disconnection dead and spiritless," are we
veering toward a newer extreme of forgetting what we
started to examine in the multitude of things seen? Is
there any method of procedure which will insure the

proper perspective? The historian and teacher of our
national letters today has to exercise the finest discrimination lest he be lured off the broad highway which
leads to his destination—a proportionate, comprehensive, balanced interpretation of American literature.

I

Present and future interpreters of American letters
must not make the easy mistake of supposing all earlier
historians dunces. Their principles, their methods, their
shortcomings, and their occasionally shrewd judgments
are often instructive, often correctives to our own
views. They deserve a brief survey before we proceed.
It is hardly necessary to dwell upon the pioneer Knapp's
abandonment of his ambitious history, or the ever-
reviving sectional pride which distorted the early pages
of Governor Bradford and Cotton Mather. Of more interest is Rufus Griswold's reply in 1847 to the jealous
upholders of "Americanism": "But there never was and
never can be an exclusively national literature. All nations are indebted to each other and to preceding ages
for the means of advancement." [1] The reaction against
the demand for a distinctive national literature is thus
by no means modern. Griswold's anthology erred in another direction—he allowed writers of the early nine-

---

[1] Introduction to *Prose Writers of America.*

teenth century to elbow their venerable forefathers out of the picture. Much better proportioned, *The Cyclopedia of American Literature* (1856) by the Duyckincks represented our literature "from the earliest period to the present day." Esthetic standards they dispensed with coolly enough to please even a social historian, holding that "it is important to know what books have been produced, and by whom; and whatever the books may have been or whoever the men."

The first true history of American literature, still unsurpassed in its field, was the four-volume work—treating the period from 1607 to 1783—by Moses Coit Tyler. This appeared between 1880 and 1897. It is especially noteworthy for its fairness, discrimination, and documentation. Unlike the majority of his successors, Tyler did not depend upon second-hand opinion. "I have endeavored," he declared austerely, "to examine the entire mass of American writings during the colonial time. . . . Upon no topic of literary estimation have I formed an opinion at second hand." [2] Literary discrimination, rather than unquestioning inclusiveness, was his ideal: "I have not undertaken to give an indiscriminate dictionary of all Americans who ever wrote anything, or a complete bibliographical account of all the Ameri-

[2] M. C. Tyler, *A History of American Literature During the Colonial Period*, 1880, Vol. I, pp. vi-vii.

can books that were ever written. It is our literary history of those writings, in the English language, produced by Americans, which have some noteworthy value as literature, and some real significance in the literary unfolding of the American mind." [3] If modern economic determinists masquerading as literary historians think he ignores to a large extent the political, religious, and social and economic backgrounds, Tyler states his justification: he regards "the proceedings of legislative bodies, the doings of cabinet ministers and of colonial politicians, the movements of armies . . . as mere external incidents." [4] He is to deal with "persons who, as mere writers, and whether otherwise prominent or not, nourished the springs of great historic events by creating and shaping and directing public opinion during all that robust time; who, so far as we here regard them, wielded only spiritual weapons; who still illustrate, for us and for all who choose to see, the majestic operation of ideas, the creative and decisive play of spiritual forces, in the development of history, in the rise and fall of nations, in the aggregation and the division of races. . . . Just what this book aims to be, then, is a presentation of the soul, rather than of the body, of the American Revolution." [5] Neglectful of im-

[3] *Op. cit.*, p. vi.
[4] M. C. Tyler, *The Literary History of the American Revolution*, 1897, Vol. I, p. vi.
[5] *Ibid.*, pp. vii-viii.

portant economic and social influences Tyler doubtless
was; but his robust faith in the power of ideals and his
recognition of the counter-influence of literature upon
historic events stand as healthful correctives to the view
of the present acquisitive age which attributes modern
motives to a more idealistic generation.

In 1892 Charles F. Richardson considered "the perspective of American Literature"—as we are here considering it—in the Introduction to his *American Literature, 1607-1885.* His main concern is that "of esti-
mating the rank and analyzing the achievements of
American authors." "Expository criticism of American
literature," he assures us, "must give way to philosophical criticism." Defining literature as "the written record
of valuable thought, having other than merely practical purpose," he concludes that "ten times" as much
space should be devoted to nineteenth century writers
as to the colonials. His work illustrates today the
peculiar futility of esthetic rankings and the neglect of
the modern fool-proof historical inquiry and explanation. However, he perhaps merits praise for his freedom
from patriotic bias, and especially for his emphasis on
a comparative method: "The critic of American literature should be thoroughly acquainted with both English
and American political, social, and literary history . . .
and yet should discriminate between variant conditions,

aims, methods, and results." "Behind literature is race; behind race, climate and environment. The history of American literature is the history of a part of the English people, under new geographical and political conditions, within the United States." Aside from its Anglo-Saxon bias, this sounds rather modern. Unfortunately, neither Professor Richardson's ability nor the contemporary knowledge of history and economics enabled him to follow out his excellent principle.

Probably one of the best of the earlier comprehensive books is Barrett Wendell's *Literary History of America* (1900). Basing his plan upon Richardson's comparative principle, Wendell surveys, for each of the three centuries, (1) English history; (2) English literature; (3) American history; and finally (4) American literature. "An important phase of our study," he maintains, "must accordingly be that which attempts to trace and to understand the changes in the native character of the Americans and of the English, which have so long resulted in disunion of national sentiment. We can scrutinize them, however, only as they appear in literary history, and mostly in that of America." [6] He makes a brave attempt at our modern methods of analysis, but unhappily he lived before the coöperative effort of the Turners and Paxsons and Schlesingers and Parringtons

[6] P. 9.

had provided the necessary materials for his work. He tries to show, for example, how "historical pressure—social, political, and economic alike" had changed the dominant type of native Englishman in the seventeenth century, while "in America there had been no such external pressure; and though isolation was making the inhabitants of New England more and more provincial, they had preserved to an incalculable degree the spontaneous, enthusiastic, versatile character of their immigrant ancestors." [7] Like Tyler's, his interpretation is predominantly idealistic: "A yearning for absolute truth, an unbroken faith in abstract ideals, is what makes distinctly national the political utterances of the American Revolution." [8] Characteristically, also, Wendell tended to see New England as the fountain-head of American literature and his own century as the fountain-head of New England. Meritorious as his general comparative plan is, he yielded to a somewhat mechanical paralleling of English and American phenomena, without demonstrating the intricate organic relations often present; and Continental literature he more or less ignored.

Professor Woodberry, in *America in Literature* (1903), perceived—as behooved a professor of com-

[7] P. 55.
[8] P. 525. Compare Parrington, *The Colonial Mind*, pp. 179 ff., for consideration of economic factors.

parative literature—the relations between European
and American romanticism, but in such a vague and
general way as to indicate slight significance. His conclusion regarding the "inadequacy of literature as a
function of national expression" [9] has been reiterated by
John Macy, in *The Spirit of American Literature*
(1913). "Our first really national period, all-American,
autochthonous"—finally found an able historian in Fred
Lewis Pattee, whose *History of American Literature
Since 1870* appeared in 1915. Sympathetic, enthusiastic,
interesting, this book treats the frontier and maintains
proper proportion, but 1870 is somewhat too late for a
thorough demonstration of the premises upon which the
book rests.

During the last few years numerous works have appeared which must be regarded as contributions to the
ideal literary history; among these, besides the earlier
epoch-making studies by Turner and other historians, one
might list such books as Foerster's *Nature in American
Literature* and *American Criticism;* Jones's *America and
French Culture;* Parrington's *Main Currents of American Thought;* the Beards' *Rise of American Civilization;*
and Hazard's *The Frontier in American Literature.*

This survey of earlier literary histories has missed its
point unless it has impressed the reader with the fact

[9] P. 205.

that most of the modern theories of approach were stated in one way or another long ago. Griswold and Richardson opposed exclusive "Americanism." Tyler stressed thoroughness and documentation. Richardson and Wendell advocated the comparative method, "English and American political, social, and literary history . . . and . . . variant conditions, aims, methods, and results." Woodberry pointed to the relation between American and European romanticism. How, then, is our modern scholarship superior, or how may it achieve superiority? First of all, we notice that the merits we have noted collectively were combined in no one history. Secondly, the early practitioners of the comparative method did not possess a sufficiently pointed, detailed knowledge of even English literature for a firm clear tracing of the pattern of western thought; they tended, also, to ignore Continental literature. Thirdly, they all display a lamentably weak grasp of the importance of economic conditions—they are over-idealistic. Environment is interpreted in the most vague manner. Indeed our most signal advantage today doubtless lies in our superior knowledge of the determining function played in American life by the constant rebirth of the frontier. Fourthly, they lived before the days of scientific scholarship, before the days of cooperative effort both in literature and in history and economics; where we would apply the inductive method in all its minute rigor, they, except perhaps Tyler, were satisfied with vague generalizations. Fifthly, they tended to use the comparative method in a rather mechanical way, paralleling national histories without a full realization of the organic relation of various trends of thought, and the flexibility of various counter-influences.

The conclusion one draws, then, from a survey of earlier histories is that their deficiency arises not so much on account of their *principles* as on account of the *methods* used. The ideal historian of American letters will therefore endeavor to combine the merits of the earlier histories while at the same time he subjects all theories to the minute, rigorous, detailed, inductive test of fact. He must refuse to generalize until the steadily increasing body of available evidence has been carefully examined. Dissertations on American literature— Masters' as well as Doctors'—should somehow be made available. The literary historian must keep abreast of the infinitely valuable investigations of his brother students in history and economics. There is a crying need for at least one learned journal devoted exclusively to publishing material bearing on American literature.[9a]

[9a] The need of which Professor Clark speaks will soon be filled by *American Literature: A Quarterly Journal of Literary History, Criticism, and Bibliography,* soon to be published by the Duke University Press with the coöperation of the American Literature Group of the Modern Language Association.—*Ed.*

Vain, scientific scholarship is so exacting that bibliographical knowledge is imperative to enable one to
avoid duplication and to build superstructures on the
basis of actual evidence massed by others. Nor must one
allow detailed scholarship to become divorced from a
broad humanistic vision and a knowledge of international movements. One point emerges clearly out of
the essays in this volume: the "blinders" must be removed from the eyes of the historian of our letters—
he must have a firm grasp on the inter-relations of literature, history, religion, economics, and social life.[10]

Various answers have been offered as to the forces
which make our letters distinctive, but the general
modern trend seems to be toward a theory of economic
determinism; this is especially apparent in the impressive interpretation of Professor Parrington,—who, Mrs.
Lucy Lockwood Hazard confesses, "first taught me the
economic interpretation of American literature." This
movement is clearly a reaction against the somewhat
one-sided idealism of Tyler and Wendell; it is also a

[10] Not only American literature, but American education in general has
suffered from a narrowly provincial method. William S. Learned in "The
Quality of the Educational Process in the United States and in Europe"—
printed in the annual reports of the Carnegie Foundation—censures the
lack of "texture or organization" in our American system. "Effective
education through related ideas is thereby sacrificed to the mere registering
of information." "In contrast," he concludes, "continuity and relationship of ideas constitute the characteristic basis of excellence in German
instruction." As a result of exhaustive research he advocates emphasis on
"Inherent relatedness and continuity of content."

sophisticated revival of Taine's deterministic theory. One might argue on general grounds that it tends to minimize the inexplicable factor of personality, that it tends to neglect the counter-determining effect of literature upon public opinion and hence upon material living; one might ask how the theory accounts for the fact that all the people, let us say, of one town, played upon by the same economic and social forces, do not produce literature, and the same sort of literature. Yet, after all, syllogistic arguments amount to little in relation to literature. The only valid test for the theory of economic determinism—or any other theory—is simply bringing the theory to the test of fact. Will the theory account for the origin of our recognized masterpieces? At any rate Professor Parrington has brought to light much valuable evidence. We need a minute study of the specific pieces of literature under consideration in relation to the background, physical, political, economic, literary, religious, and social.

## II

The relation between background and literature, between roots and flowers, is of course widely disputed, and at best one can expect agreement only as regards general method of treatment. Proportion is the objective. After a lifetime of pondering on the subject, Sir

Leslie Stephen—whose work George Meredith called "the profoundest and the most sober criticism we have had in our time"—announced: "I imagine that a literary history is so far satisfactory as it takes the facts into consideration and regards literature, in the perhaps too pretentious phrase, as a particular function of the whole social organism." Doubtless Professor Schlesinger is correct in his assertion that "To understand the literary trends of a period it thus becomes necessary to study and compare the forces at work in other cultural fields: the old geocentric attitude toward literature must yield to a more comprehensive view." It remains, however, that the student of American letters is engaged primarily in interpreting American letters, and that, while one gladly admits that his field is but part of a larger whole, and has meaning only in relation to the current trend of human society, yet the literature itself remains the true subject, and the proper focal center is finally the acknowledged masterpieces. If the literature of a certain territory or epoch is considerably below the esthetic par, but valuable as a mirror of contemporary conditions, it belongs to the field of the social historian rather than the literary historian. Speaking of the obscure writers of the Middle Western frontier, Professor Rusk says, "Their failure to realize any large measure of artistic achievement may be granted without debate."

Yet, he adds, their work is "invaluable for the record it contains of the growth of a civilization during a unique epoch." It is a "no less significant memorial of this pioneer era than are the facts of economic and political history which recent writers have so diligently explored." [11] In the nine hundred pages which constitute only two-thirds of Professor Parrington's *Main Currents in American Thought*—which a prominent authority has called "by far the best history of American literature that has yet appeared"—two and a quarter pages are devoted to Poe and two and a half to Longfellow. It is an obvious fallacy, and a dangerous sign, to favor economic determinism and then omit—or nearly omit—whatever disproves the theory. It is praiseworthy, when the facts warrant, to trace in literature a crystallization of current political, religious, social, and economic ideals. Certainly, however, one must guard against neglecting literature of a high artistic standard simply because it is not a crystallization of such events. Our literary history is perhaps suffering from a new form of sectionalism, perhaps more insidious than the old. Admitting the comparative inarticulateness—judged by literary standards—of the West and South, sectional pride has sought to supply the deficiency by neglecting work of true literary value in favor of work which obviously mirrors

[11] *The Literature of the Middle Western Frontier*, 1925, Vol. I, p. vii.

social, political, and economic conditions. This is a confusion in first principles. Dr. Henry S. Canby (*The Saturday Review*, January 8, 1927) writes: "The anti-Federalist West has saved us from the absurdity of refusing to teach our own literature, but its enthusiasm may thrust us into absurdities still more ridiculous. From curriculums in which the really important Americans are excluded while third-rate European dramatists, poets feeble by Whitman and pale by Poe, or philosophic essayists who are candles by Emerson's beam, are given tedious consideration, we are swung over into a false patriotism that gives courses in the literature of Kansas or the poets of California. Mediocre, or worse than mediocre, is brevetted if it happens to have been written in the dear old State. This is a mere disease of nationalism. . . . If we are to have sound instruction in our own literature, it must be taught as art conditioned by the American environment." We are truly concerned primarily with the history of a selection of what, judged by the timeless and international canons of art, can be called literature. And we are interested in economics and history only so far as they can be shown to have influenced directly our subject, or as they tend to clarify its direction of development. Our historical acquisitions, so valuable in many ways, should be focused upon our major literature and our major writers. One begins to wonder whether the breakdown of boundary lines between *genres* already witnessed in music, poetry, and painting is beginning to invade academic precincts. A comprehensive attempt to consider proportionately all the forces playing on literature is one thing; an attempt to teach literature as history is another. The time may come for a "newer" *Laocoön* bearing upon scholarship and teaching.

Confessing with Professor Woodberry "the inadequacy of literature as a function of national expression" when studied by itself, the literary historian still has to face the problem of an adequate and proportionate treatment of background. Does one need to master the significance of Jacksonian democracy to read intelligently "Rappaccini's Daughter"? Might one conceivably comprehend *Ben Hur* without a detailed knowledge of the intricacies of "Physiocratic agrarianism"? The background, even for the same age, varies with each book; if it amounted only to current social and economic conditions the problem would be vastly simplified. Currents of influence are infinitely complex; they may criss-cross in the same man; they may stem from any land or age. For example, to understand the forces which helped Emerson produce that slim blue edition of *Nature* one needs to know something of Emerson's protected life in quiet Concord, something, perhaps, of the influence of the spirit of the frontier which Transcendentalism reënforced; but one needs mainly to unravel the interwoven threads of Unitarianism, deism, German transcendentalism, and Platonism. Bret Harte read the Victorian Dickens in a boisterous western mining camp. Thoreau read Homer and the sages of the Orient in his hut at Walden Pond.

But to come to the point: suppose that, instead of trying to warp our literature to support the ready-made hypothesis that it is the product of current social and economic forces, we make an honest effort to approach each book or poem with an impartial mind in an attempt to ascertain inductively precisely why it is as it is and not otherwise and how it relates to current tendencies. In the study of literature, I take it, one aim somewhat neglected today is to read carefully, earnestly, and questioningly the literature itself in order to understand it, to explain its origin, and to appreciate it; for unreasoning praise is not the truest sort, and one cannot rightly admire without understanding.[12] *My central suggestion is this: suppose one focuses his attention first squarely upon the foreground—the specific book or poem under consideration; then let him view the background in this particular case through the "windows"*

[12] I refer to such rigorous reading as the ancient classics have long received. How rarely have English writers, especially of the nineteenth century, and still more rarely American writers, been subjected to a real examination!

*of the foreground.* This method has four valuable advantages: (1) it secures a proper reading of the literature itself; (2) when approached in this inductive manner the organic relation between the book and its background is more readily apparent than when one parallels in a mechanical fashion whole blocks of literature and background; (3) the amount and character of background considered in each case will be both proportionate and relevant; (4) it lends itself readily to a lively class-room discussion, inductive and Socratic, which can be climaxed in each case by a revelation of the broad significance of each book in its relation to national and European tendencies.

But the method I am advocating will be clearer, perhaps, with a few illustrations. Let us consider three poems by Philip Freneau which appear in Professor Foerster's anthology. In 1793 in the poem "On the Anniversary of the Storming of the Bastille, at Paris, July 14th, 1789," Freneau wrote:

> "Plung'd in a gulf of deep distress
> 　France turns her back—(so traitors say)
> 　Kings, priests, and nobles, round her press, . . ."
> Ye sons of this degenerate clime,
> Haste, arm the barque, expand the sail;
> Assist to speed that golden time
> When Freedom rules, and monarchs fail.

What is necessary to explain words like these? Look at Freneau's life. Neither Puritan nor Cavalier, our first poet was born in the middle colonies, of French Huguenot parentage; this in part accounts for his passion for liberty, civil as well as religious, his natural love of beauty, his robust self-reliance, his admiration for things French. He was trained at Revolutionary Princeton, "a hotbed of 'Whiggism.'" Having heartened with his poems our own Revolutionary soldiers from Valley Forge to Yorktown, he became one of the chief advocates—after the fall of the Bastille—of American aid to the French Revolutionists. Citizen Genêt was touring an enthusiastic America in 1793, an America indignant at the neutrality policy of Washington and the leading Federalists. Jacobin Clubs were organized. Sedate men of affairs wore the *bonnet rouge*. Liberty poles were raised in public places. Customs, dress, manners were *à la française*. Only French bread was tolerable. Restaurants introduced French soups, salads, ragouts, fricassees, and olive oil. The stately English minuet gave way to the lively cotillion. The streets of Philadelphia and New York were musical at night with "La Marseillaise" and the "Carmagnole." Thus Freneau's French Revolution poems simply represent a crystallization of the general social spirit of the time.

This was the period which saw the never-ending

struggle between the expansive, decentralizing French democracy of Jefferson and the aristocratic, centralizing English Federalism of Hamilton and Washington. It has been said that an understanding of the conflict between the liberty of the unionist and that of the Jeffersonian is the key which unlocks American history. The first seeks a check on the expansion of natural impulse, the other does not. A Federalist like Marshall sought to strengthen the central government by establishing the Marbury *vs.* Madison decision regarding the power of the Supreme Court to nullify an act of Congress; while Jefferson not only proclaimed human rights, but state rights, as in drafting the "Kentucky Resolutions," November, 1799. If the literature of the western world in the seventeenth century embodied a struggle between the theological and the natural man, the late eighteenth century saw the apotheosis of the natural man and natural rights. One might trace the rise of the radical movement through Hobbes, Locke, Shaftesbury, Rousseau, Condorcet, Priestley (Jefferson's friend), Paine, Godwin, and others. At this crucial time—1791 to 1793— Freneau became clerk of foreign languages for Jefferson, then Secretary of State; bits of Rousseau and the French radicals were translated for the Americans. And at the same time Freneau wielded enormous political influence as independent editor of *The National Gazette.* Opposed

to Fenno's *Gazette of the United States,* the organ of
Hamilton and the Federalists, Freneau as "the leading
editor in America" attacked the growing aristocratic,
ceremonial, centralizing tendencies and disseminated as
well the doctrines of liberty, fraternity, and equality so
dear to Rousseau, Paine, and Jefferson. The last named
confessed that Freneau "saved our Constitution, which
was fast galloping into monarchy." [13] Mr. S. E. Forman
concludes: "Freneau's paper did much to give a French
coloring to our political philosophy. . . . The editor of
*The National Gazette* was the schoolmaster who drilled
Jeffersonian or French democracy into the minds—willing or unwilling—of the American people." [14] The latest
authority on Jefferson and Hamilton remarks: "Soon
the Jeffersonian farmers in Georgia were talking what
he was writing, and Jeffersonian editors were following
his lead. In the barrooms of Rhode Island men of no
consequence were reading the paper aloud over their
mugs." [15] Social and political history has helped the
reader of Freneau to see that the poet and editor must
be considered an important agent in introducing and
popularizing the French and Jeffersonian doctrines
which later united with the frontier spirit to produce

[13] *Jefferson's Works,* Vol. I, p. 231.

[14] "The Political Activities of Philip Freneau," *Johns Hopkins University Studies in Historical and Political Science,* Series XX, p. 542.

[15] Claude G. Bowers, *Jefferson and Hamilton* (1925), p. 156.

Jacksonian democracy. For, as Professor Schlesinger admits, "Jackson himself was a product, rather than a creator of the new democratic spirit. . . ." [16] This may illustrate another point: although literature may be conditioned by the current social and political situation, it may also in turn become a power to help determine later social and political trends. Studied in a background such as this, Freneau's French Revolution poems become packed with meaning.

Let us take a second poem by Freneau, and look through another sort of "window." In his early "Power of Fancy" (1770) he expresses the contemporary attitude toward Nature:

> Ah! what is all this mighty whole,
> These suns and stars that round us roll!
> What are they all, where'er they shine,
> But Fancies of the Power Divine!
> What is this globe, these lands, and seas,
> And heat, and cold, and flowers, and trees, . . .
> But thoughts on reason's scale combin'd,
> Ideas of the Almighty mind!

If we view the background through this "window" in the foreground, we see that it is very different from that of the Puritans. Although Jonathan Edwards loved nature as a youth, he came to view it as essentially evil,

opposed to the "divine and *super*natural light"—the il-
lumination of Grace—which is God. Freneau's attitude,
on the other hand, becomes part of the deistic movement
which derived from the rationalism of Locke and Descartes, was reënforced by Shaftesbury and Bolingbroke
and Spinoza, and was versified in *The Essay on Man*
(1734):

> All are but parts of one stupendous whole,
> Whose body Nature is, and God the Soul.

Franklin and Jefferson were accused of being godless
deists. From the point of view of literature Freneau's
deism is vastly significant, for it has been demonstrated
that "deism may be said to be the starting point for our
modern treatment of nature." [17] In fact it would be
interesting to consider Freneau's deism in relation to the
claim made by Professor Pattee that "in Freneau we find
for the first time the actual life of the American
forest—the wild pink, the elm, the wild honeysuckle,
the pumpkin, the blackbird, the squirrel, the 'loquacious
whippoorwill.' " [18] Later, after deism had developed into
Unitarianism, and Emerson had resigned his Unitarian
pulpit, the Concord sage proclaimed that "to study
nature" and "to know thyself" were "the same thing," in
that both are but parts of that "Unity, that Over-Soul,

[17] C. A. Moore, "Return to Nature in the English Poetry of the
Eighteenth Century," *Studies in Philology*, Vol. XIV (1917), p. 243.
[18] *Side-Lights on American Literature*, 1922, p. 287.

within which every man's particular being is contained and made one with all other." Coleridge was a Unitarian before he became a pantheist in "The Aeolian Harp" and "Frost at Midnight." Wordsworth came to worship a god "whose dwelling is the light of setting suns," and Shelley "mixed awful talk" with his "great Parent." When men became conscious of a relationship between God and Nature, they rushed out of doors, ceased to feel that "Nature and Homer were . . . the same" and they began to write, as Wordsworth said, "with the eye on the object." In place of abstractions men like Emerson came to see that "The veritable mark of wisdom is finding the miraculous in the common"; ideas were transmuted into images as men turned to the concrete, sensuous, physical world—the true world of poetry. Thus studied in its relation to European philosophical trends, "The Power of Fancy" is fraught with significance.

Consider a third poem—"The House of Night" (1779)—which has been called "the first distinctly romantic note heard in America," a lurid poem centering about the death of Death, a churchyard, and specters.

> Dim burnt the lamp, and now the phantom Death
> Gave his last groans in horror and despair—
> "All hell demands me hence,"—he said, and threw
> The red lamp hissing through the midnight air.

What background will explain this? Plainly it has little
to do with either contemporary "physiocratic agrarianism" or deism. Seen in isolation the poem seems unique
indeed. In its proper contexture of international art,
however, it becomes part of the natural reaction against
eighteenth century rationality, convention, restraint,
and unimaginativeness—the manifestation in esthetic
terms of the spirit of independence then dominating
politics. It is part of the early romantic quest for the
grotesque, the supernatural, the horrid already manifested in Smollett's *Count Fathom* (1753), MacPherson's
"Ossian" (1760), Walpole's *Castle of Otranto* (1764),
the grim ballads by Percy (1765), and the whole grave-
yard school—Parnell, Young, Blair, the Wartons, and
others. It is unnecessary more than to mention the later
vogue of Gothic imaginings and horror in *The Mysteries of Udolpho* (1794), *Caleb Williams* (1794),
Shelley's *Zaztrozzi* (1810), Mrs. Shelley's masterly
*Frankenstein* (1818), or the American *Wieland*
(1798), and "Fall of the House of Usher" (1840). Even
before "The House of Night" Freneau had written "Pictures of Columbus," dealing with an enchantress who
surrounds herself with snakes, toads, winding sheets,
dead men's bones and ghosts. Now if literature is but
one manifestation of the spirit of an age, we should
expect to find parallel developments in other arts such

as painting and architecture. Nor shall we be mistaken. Washington Allston's paintings included "Dead Men Revived by Touching Elisha's Bones" (1811); "Belshazzar's Feast, or the Hand Writing on the Wall"; "Jacob's Dream" (1817); "Saul and the Witch of Endor" (1831) and "Spaletro's Vision of the Bloody Hand" (1831)—titles which speak for themselves. Rembrandt Peale painted the "Ascent of Elijah" (1812) and the "Court of Death" (1820). About 1814 John Singleton Copley did a "Resurrection." "Death on a Pale Horse" (1825) by Dunlap was an imitation of Benjamin West's similar subject. The same rebellion against correctness, symmetry and formality appears in architecture, both in England and America. About the middle of the eighteenth century in England the classical style of Inigo Jones and Sir Christopher Wren had to compete with the growing taste for Gothic castles and abbeys, as witnessed in Walpole's Ginger Bread Castle at Strawberry Hill and Backford's gloomy model of the Hall of Eblis with its three hundred foot tower at Fonthill. These were chapters in romanticism written in wood and mortar. Greek pediments, the classic orders, and symmetry gave way to towers, pinnacles, pointed arches, and all sorts of irregularity. In America Jefferson proposed some Gothic models as early as 1771, but the actual revival began in 1800 when a Gothic country house was built near Philadelphia. In 1807 a Gothic chapel appeared in Baltimore, and from 1812 on church architecture became increasingly Gothic. Thus the background viewed through the "window" of "The House of Night" is of a still different order: it locates Freneau in the pattern of "Gothic" art which was developing in England, Germany, France, and America.

Yet some of our greatest literature has been conditioned by—and is to some extent the crystallization of—the American environment. Turn for a moment to *Moby Dick* by Herman Melville, whom John Freeman—his English-Men-of-Letters biographer—regards as "the most powerful of all the great American writers." Even as late as 1892 Richardson could dismiss Melville in half of one paragraph as known merely for "adventurous rapidity of description of Pacific seas, ships, savages, and whales." [19] It was as a romance of the sea that *Moby Dick* won fame, and probably the great majority of ardent admirers today ignore its profound symbolism. As every one today knows, it is the story of the search for a white whale by a mad sea captain—Ahab—who had lost one of his legs in the whale's jaws. It is a book packed with thrilling adventure, realistic detail, "blubber and mysticism," vivid pictures of the Pacific, humor and irony, living and

[19] *American Literature, 1607-1885* (1892), p. 404.

shadowy characters, color. At the last, the whale is en-
countered and after a terrific struggle sinks the vessel
and all are lost except Ishmael, teller of the tale.

Let us view the background through this "window."
What accounts for the framework of the book and its
power as a work of art? History can help us. In early
New England the sea was both an economic escape and
a romantic adventure. *Moby Dick* is a crystallization of
the ingrained New England love of the sea, just as *The
Last of the Mohicans* is a crystallization of the love of
the frontier. Burke had bade his haughty colleagues
"look at the manner in which the people of New England have of late carried on the whale fishery. . . . No
sea but what is vexed by their fisheries. No climate that
is not a witness to their toils." [20] It was in the midst of
this great period that Melville lived. In his day, of
course, the West was not yet opened to any great extent,

[20] The Beards write: "The inhospitable soil of New England early
directed the industry of the Puritans to the sea, to fishing, shipping,
trading and all the varied interests connected with such undertakings.
Local forests furnished oak for timbers and boards, fir for masts, pitch
for turpentine and tar; fields yielded rope for hemp; and mines iron
for anchors and chains. Why should man be a serf of the soil when he
could ride the bounding main? . . . Sea breezes carried them into distant lands where they saw strange peoples and stranger customs which
slowly dissolved in skepticism the faith and usages of their fathers. . . .
Out of the oil and candles yielded by this dangerous pursuit flowed a
huge business with the mother country and Europe. Under the glow of
oil lamps, the cottages of New England farmers were transformed at night
from dingy hovels into well-lighted homes where books could be read
and games played after the long day's work was done—a novel and appealing scene in the history of agriculture, and the beginning of a revolution in culture." *Rise of American Civilization* (1927), Vol. I, pp. 90-92.

and the sea was the main avenue for adventure. As a result of the Napoleonic Wars our sea-power increased rapidly after 1800; it reached its peak in the decade following 1840. It declined before the Civil War on account of the Gold Rush of '49 and the opening of the West. The Civil War hurt our shipping, and the advent of iron ships destroyed the profit of our wooden ship manufactories. The point to remember is that Melville was fortunate enough to go to sea during the golden age of whalers, during the picturesque glory of the clipper ship; he was fortunate enough to crystallize into one book—as a cloak for his metaphysics—the romance of the era of our greatest shipping when men's minds were captivated by tales of strange deeds done on remote seas.

*Moby Dick* is, however, more than a picturesque travel book: it is a spiritual epic, of profound symbolism all compact. "Yes, the world's a ship on its passage out, and not a voyage complete." "All evil, to crazy Ahab, were visibly personified, and made practically assailable in Moby-Dick." The struggle is symbolized between the eternal ruthlessness of nature and the enmity of man. At the end, Ahab cries, as he sinks, "Towards thee I roll, thou all-destroying but conquering whale; to the last I grapple with thee; from hell's heart I stab at thee; for hate's sake I spit my last breath at thee. . . . Thus I give up the spear." Malignant forces rule the universe.

Viewing the background, once more, through this "window," what do we see? It is significant that *Moby Dick* (1851) comes after a period of religious speculation—Unitarianism and Transcendentalism. Both had stressed the infinite possibilities of man and the beneficence of the universe. In *Mardi* (1849) Melville—like Shelley in "Alastor" (1816) and "Epipsychidion" (1821)—had pursued an incarnate ideal in the futile quest for the dream-maiden Yillah, who symbolizes Unattainable Beauty, "the earthly semblance of my earliest thoughts"; it was the quest of Novalis for the "blue flower" on Puritan and pioneer soil. Transcendentalism had inspired Melville with visions of more spacious horizons, human and divine, and it had taught him, after the German Fichte, that his own soul was the heart of those horizons. Emerson still lectured sweetly on optimism, compensation, and a beneficent universe. Carlyle was still hoarsely trumpeting his transcendentalism across the Atlantic. But there were signs of change. Byron's Cain, torn by a conflict between Calvinistic fatalism and the transcendental and humanitarian might of the individual mind, had dared to "look the Omnipotent tyrant in his Everlasting face, and tell him that His evil is not good!" Even Thoreau, part naturalist, the disciple of Emerson, is in *Walden* (1854) "conscious of an animal in us, which awakens in proportion as our higher nature slumbers. It is reptile and sensual, and perhaps cannot be wholly expelled. . . . Nature is hard to be overcome, but she must be overcome." Melville had married in 1847, had lived for three years in New York, and then retired for thirteen years to a farmhouse near Pittsfield, Massachusetts. A few miles away, in the Red Cottage in Lenox, Hawthorne wrote: "On the hither side of Pittsfield sits Herman Melville, shaping out the gigantic conception of his 'white whale,' while the gigantic shadow of Greylock looms upon him from his study window." Here Melville pondered, trying to reconcile his tender transcendental dreams with the cruelty of nature he had seen with his own eyes from the forecastle of the whaler *Acushnet*. He recalls basking aloft in the rigging of the ship: he "takes the mystic ocean at his feet for the visible image of that deep, blue, bottomless soul, pervading mankind and nature. . . . But while this sleep, this dream is on ye, move your hand or foot an inch; slip your hand at all: your identity comes back in horror. Over Descartian vortices you hover. And perhaps, at midday, in the fairest weather, with one half-throttled shriek, you drop through that transparent air into the summer sea, no more to rise for ever. Heed it

well, ye Pantheists." In Melville's mind, ingrained
transcendental optimism, with its serene faith in a
beneficent nature, clashed with his first-hand knowledge
of a nature—as Tennyson was saying at the same time—
"red in tooth and claw." Out of the conflict Ahab was
born. But had this conflict not taken place in the mind
of a man who had gone to sea in precisely this brilliant
and picturesque period we have described, we should
have, undoubtedly, a book of metaphysics instead of
what has been called "the New England *Faust.*" We see
*Moby Dick,* therefore, as an embodiment of a world
trend in thought—a protesting recoil from the extrava-
gances of romantic thought—which is conditioned by
and partly the result of a definite "block" of American
environment.[21]

Perhaps I have done enough to make clear my main
contention: that background, both European and
American, is of the utmost importance in interpreting
American literature in its larger significance. But it
must not be allowed to obliterate the foreground, the

[21] If space permitted, it would be interesting to consider, similarly,
the relation between Mark Twain's story of "The Celebrated Jumping Frog
of Calaveras County" and the jubilant, reckless, optimistic West of 1867.
One might go on to contemplate the growing cynicism with which the
"£1,000,000 Bank Note" (1893) mirrors a later society which bows down
in reverence to nothing but money. And one might measure Mark Twain
as a critic of an acquisitive society in "The $30,000 Bequest," which
reflects the corroding effect of avarice on a society which was in 1904
suffering from the megalomania and imperialism which is part of our
heritage from a Jeffersonian and Jacksonian democracy which we saw
Freneau helping to advance.

literature itself. Our major literature should be made the center round which historical study should play. As a means of securing a proportionate and relevant background, I have tried to illustrate the advantages of viewing it through the windows of the foreground—through a careful and intelligent reading of the literature itself. Furthermore, this consideration of collateral manifestations of the time-spirit helps to clarify and verify the general trend in literature of American life. It also aids us to plot with some degree of accuracy the curve of our probable development. And when literature is studied from this point of view the American people may be able to direct the future with more wisdom. In the life of the past, as mirrored in literature, there exists a reasonable and dependable guide for a troubled present, a guide which it is one of the higher functions of scholarship to render available.

NOTE.  For courteous permission to make quotations in the foregoing chapter from copyrighted books I am indebted as follows: to Thomas Y. Crowell Company, publishers of Hazard's *The Frontier in American Literature*; to G. P. Putnam's Sons, publishers of Tyler's *A History of American Literature, 1607-1765*, *A Literary History of the American Revolution*, and Richardson's *American Literature, 1607-1885*; to Charles Scribner's Sons, publishers of Wendell's *A Literary History of America*; to Macmillan Company, publishers of Schlesinger's *New Viewpoints in American History*, the Beards' *The Rise of American Civilization*, and Freeman's *Herman Melville*; to the Century Company, publishers of Pattee's *Side-Lights on American Literature* and *A History of American Literature since 1870*; to the Columbia University Press, publishers of Rusk's *The Literature of the Middle Western Frontier*; to Dr. Henry Canby, editor of *The Saturday Review*; to Houghton Mifflin Company, publishers of Bowers' *Hamilton and Jefferson*; and to Harper and Brothers, publishers of Woodberry's *America in Literature*.